FED WAY REG

SEP 1 9 2004

APR   2004

CALIFORNIA COTTAGE STYLE

CALIFORNIA
COTTAGE STYLE

ANN & SCOT ZIMMERMAN

STERLING PUBLISHING CO., INC. NEW YORK
A STERLING/CHAPELLE BOOK

CHAPELLE, LTD.:
  Jo Packham
  Sara Toliver
  Cindy Stoeckl

Editor: Laura Best
Art Director: Karla Haberstich
Copy Editor: Marilyn Goff

Staff: Kelly Ashkettle, Areta Bingham,
Donna Chambers, Ray Cornia, Emily Frandsen,
Lana Hall, Susan Jorgenson, Barbara Milburn,
Lecia Monsen, Suzy Skadburg, Kim Taylor,
Desirée Wybrow

If you have any questions or comments, please contact:
          Chapelle, Ltd., Inc.,   P.O. Box 9252, Ogden, UT 84409
          (801) 621-2777 • (801) 621-2788 Fax
          e-mail: chapelle@chapelleltd.com   web site: chapelleltd.com

Library of Congress Cataloging-in-Publication Data

Zimmerman, Ann.
   California cottage style / Ann & Scot Zimmerman.
      p. cm.
   "A Sterling/Chapelle Book."
   Includes bibliographical references and index.
   ISBN 1-4027-0387-2
1. Cottages--California. 2. Country homes--California. I. Zimmerman,
Scot. II. Title.
NA7561.Z56 2003
728'.37'09794--dc21

                                        2003009346

10 9 8 7 6 5 4 3 2 1
Published by Sterling Publishing Co., Inc.
387 Park Avenue South, New York, NY 10016
©2003 by Ann & Scot Zimmerman
Distributed in Canada by Sterling Publishing
c/o Canadian Manda Group,
One Atlantic Avenue, Suite 105
Toronto, Ontario, Canada M6K 3E7
Distributed in Great Britain by Chrysalis Books
64 Brewery Road, London N7 9NT, England
Distributed in Australia by Capricorn Link (Australia) Pty. Ltd.
P.O. Box 704, Windsor, NSW 2756, Australia
Printed in China
All Rights Reserved
Sterling ISBN 1-4027-0387-2

Cottages reflect a time, a place, and a need for shelter, as well as the available building materials and the traditions and collective memories of their builders and owners.

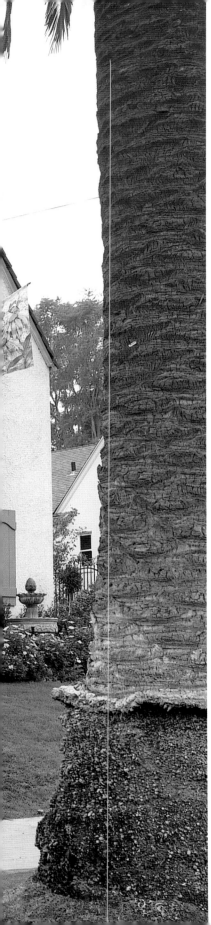

TABLE OF CONTENTS

PREFACE
WHAT MAKES A HOME A COTTAGE?

Say the word "cottage" and it evokes a modest, charmingly imperfect, whimsical home tucked among raucously blooming flowers. We imagine the comfortable interior to be filled with painted furniture, embroidered linens, stenciled walls, and well-loved treasures created by generations of talented hands. The only sounds that come through the open casement windows are the songs of birds and the laughter of children. Thanks to the detailed illustrations of childhood fairy tales and stories, cottages have become images of myth and magic, like sanctuaries in the woods with roses covering whitewashed walls and thatched roofs.

What defines a house as a cottage? Strictly speaking, a cottage is defined in dictionaries as a small, usually wood-frame, one-family home typically occupied by a worker or rural laborer. Through time, small homes for vacation use have similarly been christened cottages. Now the term "cottage" can be loosely applied to modestly sized vacation homes. Guidelines for identifying a cottage are a thousand square feet or less, no more than two stories, and six or fewer main rooms. Some glossaries and writers find exceptions to even these generous guidelines. Interestingly, few books on cottages ever set forth a definition, which increased the importance of making this my starting point in portraying a California Cottage Style.

These definitions were somewhat sterile compared to the romantic images I formed as a child of vine-covered cottages with steaming pies on freshly painted windowsills. Images like these were repeated in the stories my grandmother read or made up, hoarsely whispering them to my brother and I as we sat motionless at each side of her. We listened as she told her tales with a heavy accent and mint-scented breath of simple, cheerful, beautiful cottages where often miracles happened to desperate but decent and well-meaning people. Wanting to know more about the traditions of cottages that appear in my grandmother's stories and other literature led to a several-day search. It was with a stack of architectural, home, and history books that I started to discover the sources and traditions of cottage style and design.

I first found a historical trail for cottages in English tradition, then followed it forward to America where it continued across the nation. Few cottages built in England before the 17th century have survived. Remnants indicate these early cottages were built from sticks and mud, with low ceilings and one room—windowless so smoke from the fire escaped through the door. They were simple structures, just a small step better than huts, that took only a few days to build. People slept in the cottages but cooked and worked outdoors; and their gardens were utilitarian rather than decorative. On larger farms in some areas, the entire household was enclosed in the same building. This building included one section for farm animals and another for people. All the members

"Hansel" by Hugh Comstock
Carmel, California

9

of the household—field workers, servants and family—slept in the same one or two rooms.

After 1600AD, cottages became more permanent structures, indicating that cottage dwellers were experiencing greater prosperity than before. Traditions changed so that it was common for farm families to have their own homes. Oftentimes families supplemented their incomes with side businesses operated from their cottages, such as chair-turning, lace-making, nail-making, spinning, and weaving, giving rise to the term "cottage industries."

Rural cottages typically had a steep ladder leading up from two or more rooms on the ground floor to the loft or floors above, which evolved sometimes to spiral stairs or a half-course of stairs with a turn. Hoods made from mud and eventually fireplace stacks made from more enduring materials vented smoke.

In contrast to grand houses that began to appear in the 18th century, cottage headroom was low, the size was small, and few cottages featured decoratively carved stone or timber. Cottage designs and construction methods at this time were "vernacular"—meaning cottages were built not by specialists but by local people according to local traditions and with the materials that were available close by. The design traditions varied by area as home builders learned techniques from one another. At that time the canal and road systems had not been fully developed, so materials imported from other areas were rare. Thus different regional cottage-building and design styles evolved.

In forested areas, one of the early building methods was timber frame. This had many variations according to local traditions. Methods included cruck timbers, where large timbers inclined and their tops joined at the apex in a wishbone formation; post and truss; and box framing. Box framing had its own variations of large framing, small framing, and close studding. To visualize early tim-

ber frame, think of the buildings in sets for Elizabethan plays. The support structure remains exposed on the exterior. The dark timbers contrast to the light color of the limestone mixture that covered the panels within the timber frame—wattle and daub. To make wattle, light vertical timber was woven with slender branches and reeds, and these were covered with daub—a mixture of clay, dung, and chopped straw. Over time, alternatives were developed to wattle and daub. These include brick noggin (filling in with decorative bricks), and lime plaster over mud and stave.

Additionally, during the period between 1600 and the mid 1700s, cottages flourished that were built from materials other than timber frame. In areas with few forests, locals built cottages of available natural materials such as stone, unbaked earth-turf, and cob (clay, straw, chalk and small stones.) By the 18th century, bricks made an appearance and makers of cottages introduced techniques like "tumbling in" for strength and irregular shapes and textures. Also new in the 18th century was the introduction of glass. Roof finishes were thatch, stone slates, clay tiles, clay pantiles, and shingles.

"Bonner House"
Victorian Period Gothic Revival
Midway, Utah

England's population underwent significant changes between 1750 and 1800. These changes in turn affected the cottage styles. The population grew by half—from six million to nine million, while at the same time income rose substantially. The social structure also changed, leading to the formation of larger estates along with a desire to display wealth and taste. The majority of people still lived in the country, so there was a need to build more cottages faster when the population increased. Better transportation in the form of roads and canals became available in the late 18th century. With the move to industrialization, centrally manufactured bricks were stronger and more regular in shape. Use of these bricks began during this period, but reached its height in the middle of the 19th century. As they became more affordable, bricks became more common in cottages owned by people of lesser means.

During the Georgian Polite period (roughly 1750–1815) owners of estates began to build cottages that were intended for more than just shelters for their workers. They looked upon the scenes of their estates like paintings, and cottages were carefully sited and decoratively designed to complement the landscape as a picturesque ideal fitting to a period in which nostalgia and natural order and harmony were valued. This is the point at which professionals began to design and build cottages for estate owners, and the term that was applied to these structures is "Polite." Designers incorporated different vernacular styles as a nostalgic ideal for a romanticized past of pastoral simplicity. Books and pattern books such as Nathaniel Kent's in 1775 (as described by Christopher Powell) confirmed the picturesque ideal. The Picturesque cottage style presented in these books departed from the earlier practicality of the working classes and included: intricacy, variety, play of outline, asymmetrical positioning, porches, overhanging eaves, recessed windows, large intricate chimneys, and gardens with creepers, shrubs, and trees.

Popular designers wrote texts to explain their designs. Kent's pattern book sets standards for headroom, stairs instead of ladders, ground floor finishes instead of the dirt in the cottages that preceded, and goals for health, warmth, comfort, and light. According to Kent, cottages should be perfectly situated in the landscape,

left: "Sticks & Stones" Carmel, California

extravagant ornamentation in an effort to touch the emotions. These cottages were built by people of means with the intention of reinforcing the ideal or the identity of the estate. They were also intended to be escape destinations to enjoy the simplicity and pastoral health of the country. The style of some cottages replicated the great house and other buildings on the estate. Another practice was to turn to classical architectural style, which was enjoying a revived interest during "The Age of Reason." Cottages Ornées were frequently sited near a town and close to the benefits of society, and many see them as the precursors to second homes and suburban-style living. During this period, cottage style was broadened to include elements from the Picturesque style. This carried to the Victorian Polite

preferably near a neighbor to help one out in times of troubles. According to Powell, in 1798 James Malton advocated a cottage style with irregular breaks in the direction of walls, one point being higher than the other, and a wide variety of roofing and walling materials. To some, the design of Picturesque cottages became almost a caricature of the preceding vernacular cottages as the designs searched for an ideal of contented cheerfulness and balance between nature and man.

From the Picturesque period for the first time came a professional architectural style particular to cottages, and this in turn leads to the Cottages Ornées. Stepping beyond the Picturesque, the goal for Cottages Ornées was to start with a modest building structure and add period cottage designs that emphasized ornamental gables, chimneys, dormers, decorative finials, and lattice-casement windows. From the period of the Cottages Ornées came a lasting association for cottages as cheerful and independent structures and as vacation getaways, along with a tinge of being sentimental and escapist.

The next evolution for cottage design came during the period of Victorian Vernacular/Victorian Polite (1815–1875). It was during this period that American designers and writers popularized cottages in America and laid the groundwork for California cottage style. While the Picturesque and Cottages Ornées movements focused more on the exteriors, siting, and ornamentation, this period brought attention to the interior spaces and cottages' livability. Cottages became home to a new class of workers who linked farms to industry. These new laborers were blacksmiths, carters, cobblers, and wheelwrights as well as miners and industrial workers. In contrast to the past, worker cottages were built with universal building methods and materials brought close to the locations by railroads, ending most local vernacular cottage-building traditions. In addition, this period spawned reformist thinking and new interest in ventilation, water supply, waste disposal, and public decency.

These themes were picked up by designers of the time. Powell reports that in 1816 Richard Elsam focused on hygiene and morality in his pattern book, when he advocated a spacious and ventilated main room with a roomy and comfortable fireplace. Powell's historical account continues: In 1833, in his book *Encyclopedia of Cottage, Farm and Villa Architecture*, John Loudon advocated providing gardens and land allotments for worker cottages in order that they may grow fresh food. In 1849 J. Young McVicar specified entrance porches, a scullery, a living room, and three bedrooms for cottages in order to separate children by sexes and eliminate the tradition of unrelated people sleeping in the same room, which offended the heightened moral sensibilities of the time more than in the past. For the more affluent, the tradition of the Cottages Ornées continued for country residences, and pattern books carried floor plans and designs that were emulated.

In America, Andrew Jackson Downing, known as his country's first great landscape designer, brought pattern books and an American cottage ideal to a waiting public at a time when the country was expanding with farms, towns, and settlements. In Downing's widely distributed book *Victorian Cottage Residences*, first published in 1842, he urged anyone living in the country to be familiar with domestic architecture, and he set a goal for American-built homes to rival the cottage homes of

England. As a landscape designer, he went further than some of the English pattern books and pressed his readers to look upon the home and gardens as an "agreeable whole." In his patterns he went so far as to design the gardens with recommendations for specific plants along side with the traditional elements of floor plans, elevations, and a description of building materials. Consistent with Victorian Period philosophies, he associated a good cottage design and well-kept gardens as a moral good, "What an unfailing barrier against vice, immorality, and bad habits are those tastes which lead us to embellish a home, to which at all times and in all places we turn with delight, as being the object and the scene of our fondest cares, labors, and enjoyments; whose humble roof, whose shady porch, whose verdant lawn and smiling flowers, all breathe forth to us, in true, earnest tones, a domestic feeling that at once purifies the heart, and binds us more closely to our fellow-beings!" Through this period numerous pattern books prospered, including Downing's two that have been revived in print, *American Victorian Cottage Homes* by Palliser, Palliser & Co., 1878, and *Later Victorian Houses and Cottages, Floor Plans and Illustrations for 40 House Designs*, The Century Architectural Company, 1897.

The lengthy Victorian period popularized and revived a number of design styles. In his cottage book just discussed, Downing included cottages that were in the styles of Rural Gothic, Classical (Greek), chateau, Swiss, Rustic Pointed, Rhine, Elizabethan, Pointed, Tuscan, Italian, Gate Lodge, and Old English. There was an equal variation in the materials he specified for construction (brick, stick, stone, wood frame). Later, other styles prospered, especially the popular Queen Anne style. This range of styles rivals some contemporary subdivisions; but at that time, many cottages were intended to be isolated and set off from other homes in the country. The most dramatic examples of Victorian architecture that survive today (because these are often the focus of preservation efforts) are large manor homes, estates, and city homes for the prominent and well-to-do. These surviving cottages may reflect the styles of the current time, but unfortunately, few have been preserved to their original period or are open for tours.

Few cottages of the day were architecturally designed. These cottages were usually larger overall commissions where the cottages were intended to blend with a theme for the main house

"Green" Bungalow
Palo Alto, California

or the estate. It was more common for cottage designs to be copied from pattern books, for builders to base them on other projects they had built, or for cottages to be designed to capture a memory or an image of another home and another place. The tradition continued, too, for workers and people of modest means to build their own homes or to enlist some temporary help from itinerate craftsmen. At the same time, railroads, mines, and factories built simple cottages to house workers that featured little ornamentation.

By the mid 1800s, the cottage traditions that appeared in my grandmother's stories had been firmly established. These traditions carried with them a sense of intimate shelter with simplicity and purity of living based on moral righteousness and, almost paradoxically, a sense of escapism and romance for rediscovering nature and retreating from worldliness. By tradition, cottage gardens nourished the spirits as well as filled the table, and were inseparably linked to the design of the home.

Cottage design elements that had origins in the limited building materials and vernacular building traditions were refined and broadened so that by the time my grandmother told me the story of the pie cooling on the cottage windowsill, I envisioned in my mind a vivid picture that had been cultivated during the two preceding centuries—there were deep overhangs, the cottage was airy and sunny, the windows were casement, the chimney was prominent and decorative, and there were hollyhocks, hydrangeas, and peonies outside the window.

The Victorian and English cottage traditions were firmly planted when Americans rushed to California for gold in 1849. Once a family became established, cottages were the preferred residences for a modest, decent lifestyle. Pattern books presented designs that incorporated aspects of European countryside vernacular with traditional styles from the Picturesque and Cottages Ornées movements as well as the standards for hygiene and decency, greater spaciousness, and popular design styles from the Victorian Period. American traditions stressed an ornamental garden to complement the style of the home along with continuing the traditions of kitchen and vegetable gardens.

Like many of the traditions in California, tracing the habitude of cottages is a jagged path. Before the Europeans (Cabrillo in 1542, Sir Francis Drake in 1579) arrived in California, there were more than 100 different Native American tribes living there. The Spanish founded a string of missions starting with San Diego in 1769, and the Russians built Fort Ross in 1812 to protect their claim from the Spanish. In 1823 the Mexican government overthrew the Spanish and established a seat of government in Sonoma. United States traders and settlers poured in during the 19th century, and in 1846 they staged Bear Flag revolt against the Mexican government. A year later, the United States government took over.

There were less than 100,000 people counted in the 1850 California census, and this grew to over 33 million a 150 years later, making California's 155,973 square miles the most populous state in the United States. Through the 150 years of mass immigration, people took westward their traditions of home and comfort, including those inherited from abroad. As a result, eclectic is the rule rather than the exception. Spanish-tiled courtyards and homes, casitas, steep-roofed Tudors, California Bungalows, and square modern minimalist homes sit along the same residential street. Likewise, California's geography offers a variety of climates, ranging from the hot dry Mojave Desert, the coolness of the highest mountain peaks in the Continental United States, the Mediterranean-like climate in northern California, and the temperate climate of the most productive agricultural valley in the world. In cottages, the range and variation in style, decor, and location are enormous.

Cottages carry an early tradition of self-sufficiency, homemade goods, and retreats for artists and writers. The scale, whimsey, and creativity of craft art meld well with chintz and cottage furniture. Also by tradition, hand-me-down furniture can be blended into the whole with the help of a common coat of paint or the addition of a

"Sticks & Stones"
Carmel, California

common brightly printed fabric. Like the rest of America, California has a long tradition of craft art, including the California College of Arts and Crafts in Oakland and San Francisco, which was founded in 1907. The Arts and Crafts architectural movement was also strongly rooted in California as Bernard Maybeck designed shingled houses for professors in the Berkeley hills at the turn of the 20th Century, and Charles and Henry Greene based their practice in southern California in 1893. California has an equally strong tradition of fine artists. Just as Americans immigrated west to the warm weather and Pacific Ocean of California, so did artists, writers, dramatists, and other creative people who made their mark on the culture. Evidence is the film industry in Hollywood, the Beat Movement in San Francisco, the photographers, artists, and writers based in Carmel, and the photographers in Yosemite and Big Sur. Similarly, in the late 1940s and 1950s, portions of the intellectual movement that had been in centered in Paris in the 1920s moved to New York, then relocated again in Los Angeles, reinforcing California as an international cultural center. The social and antiwar movement that included submovements of living closer to nature and self-sufficiency had its strongest roots initially in California. Now California is rich with museums and galleries that feature the paintings, sculptures, and environmental art of adopted and native sons and daughters. Similarly ceramics, jewelry, wood, glass, and

19

fabric studios dot the landscape, and fill galleries and specialty stores.

Cottages continue to be vacation destinations that follow the tradition of the Cottages Ornées, and the tradition has gathered a mystique of romance. Many honeymooners and couples who are still embarking on a lifetime honeymoon find cottages to be right for quiet hours together. Beyond the cozy sense of shelter and enclosure are the gardens, fragrances, natural settings, windows open to moonlight, simplicity, and other endearing details that punctuate the memories of closeness and intimacy.

By tradition, cottages are homes in which the working underpinnings of a household are visible—hanging cooking utensils, washboards, and cooling loaves of baked bread on the counter. Picturesque cottages during the 18th century were perfectly sited in the most picturesque locations to resemble paintings, and so can be cottage-vacation destinations of today. Cottages carry the tradition of reminding us to live well, in beauty, and close to nature. Because the cottage tradition is a small home on a large lot with a big garden, as the value of the land increases, sadly there is greater pressure to raze old cottages for larger homes. Preservation groups and cottage lovers have their hands full to resist such strong economic and development pressures.

Cottages have long demonstrated living simply but beautifully. With the renewed interest in living well in smaller homes, they provide examples for space planning and organization. They show how less floor space concentrates resources to make a home that is comfortable, well crafted, and personal. Usually every square foot of a well-loved cottage is graced with attentive details and, in turn, the home nurtures its occupants. In a small space, it is possible for light to come from two or three sides and stay cheery as the sun moves its course.

Details like bay windows, nooks, sloping ceilings, in addition to the cozy size, easily make a home intimate and warm. There is a revival in cottage construction as urban infill. The size fits with the scale of older neighborhoods, and they are also more affordable because of their size and the construction materials. The social faces of cottages with their front porches and richness of windows promote neighborhood interaction, thus helping to build a sense of community.

California has traditions of cottages as settler homes, worker residences, artist and writer sanctuaries, starter homes, vacation getaways, and as private spaces on large hotel properties. Through these pages you can gain a glimpse of simple creative living that is graced by openness to worldly inspirations of beauty, from the humble to the most sophisticated. Many of the featured cottages in the chapters that follow trace California's traditional building styles—Pioneer, Stick, Queen Anne, Spanish Colonial Revival, Craftsman (Bungalow), and the English and Tudor Revivals. Perhaps the most endearing and interesting are

the reemerging Romantic Picturesque and the vernacular cottages. Faced with a site, materials, and a desire for simple shelter, people have come up with ingenious and endearing cottage homes. This book is just a sampler or a taste of California's cottage styles. With it, you can understand the duel forces, as one resident phrased it, of the charm and challenges of cottage living.

The pages that follow are graced with my husband Scot's photographs of well-loved cottages in nine different California communities. Through these photographs and the accompanying text, we hope to show how these cottages reflect a time, a place, and a need for shelter, as well as the available building materials and the traditions and collective memories of their builders and owners. It is our hope that these cottages will inspire the readers, as they did us, in the art of living small and well, which is the heart of cottage style.

A Victorian vacation cottage St. Helena, California

Ann Getz Zimmerman

21

This symmetrical cottage style is said to be East Coast Colonial, with Dutch influences that are found in the curved forms on the front of the porch and in the interior stairway and ceiling details.

FORTY-NINERS' COTTAGE
HEALDSBURG

Many California settlers built cottages in the tradition of the Victorian era. Unfortunately, few of the original cottage homes have survived, and fewer are in recognizable condition due to remodeling and deterioration. After years of neglect, the Henry Gillespie/Marion Bates cottage in Healdsburg needed much more than a facelift to stave off the advances of age when Dana DiRicco initiated a rescue. She had loved the home since playing across the street in the schoolyard as a child. DiRicco, a third-generation local resident, holds double degrees in engineering and construction management and training in historical preservation. The other half of this restoration partnership is her husband, Dr. Glenn Benjamin, a veterinarian specializing in large and exotic animals. As a man who has faced many tormented elephants, lions, and buffalo, he fears little, including formidable restorations. Together DiRicco and Benjamin committed to bringing the cottage back to its original form.

Healdsburg, a picturesque town built along the Russian River, is now known for its fine wineries. The town center is a square park surrounded by grid streets, a design that remains as a tribute to the town's founder, Harmon Heald, who came west from Ohio to mine gold.

Seven years after the founding of the town, former gold miner Henry Gillespie built this clapboard cottage from redwood for his bride, Marion Bates. The cottage is one of Healdsburg's surviving "Old Ladies," a local term for homes built within 10 years of the founding of the town.

Gillespie, like other builders of Healdsburg's early cottages, was not a professional builder and constructed the home from readily available materials. The lumber used in construction tells the age of the home, since 10 feet was the maximum length that could be cut by the circular saw of the local mill. It was not until the arrival of the Northern Pacific Railroad to Healdsburg in 1871 that lumber was available in longer lengths.

The original charm of the cottage and garden has been fully restored. The short front lot is perfect for a cottage garden that is filled with blooming plants and no lawn. In the back, in keeping with Healdsburg history as a fruit-growing area, the yard features several varieties of fig, pear, apple, and citrus trees.

The deodar cedar in the right-front garden is listed as a Heritage Tree, and is documented as having been planted by noted horticulturalist Luther Burbank. Tours frequently gather to see the tree, which attracts as much attention as the cottage.

The cottage illustrates some of the fashions and decorations of the mid-Victorian period. In furnishing the home, DiRicco concentrated on the period when Bates' son occupied the home and selected furnishings, linens, rugs, and artwork consistent to both the period and the place.

above: Long views, such as these into the kitchen on the left and the master bedroom in the right, are a way to achieve a feeling of spaciousness in a cottage or small home.

right: Because of its history as a vacation and weekend spot for wealthy San Franciscans, Healdsburg offers many opportunities to acquire antiques and collectibles such as this selection of linens, silver, and Haviland china.

Saving the cottage was not a small undertaking after years of disrepair. The couple started by repairing the foundation, replacing the roof, sanding the floors, and peeling off paint and wallpaper. When it was ready for furnishing, DiRicco's love for the Victorian era surfaced. She outfitted the cottage with Victorian period furniture that she had begun to collect 20 years before.

Virginia Woolf called out in her famous essay that a woman needs a room of her own, but DiRicco argues that for her, a cottage of her own is so much the better. After the hard work of restoration, she reserves the cottage for regular afternoon teas with friends, offers it as a pied-à-terre for family living nearby, and occasionally rents it to weekenders. Locally she has found paintings by listed artists and a variety of Tiffany china and silver.

The parlor and dining room enjoy ample windows on three sides for excellent natural light throughout the day. DiRicco selected some locally significant furniture for the parlor of her cottage. The paired red parlor chairs once belonged to General Mariano Vallejo, first Governor of California and the brother-in-law of the landowner of early Healdsburg. The secretary on the left belonged to Chief Justice Searles, the first to hold that position in California.

26

right: The painted, curved wooden-slat ceiling, carved moldings, vintage-reproduction wallpaper, antiques, and handmade lace in the master bedroom take you back to a much slower-paced time.

below: Through the paned vertical-casement windows and lace curtains, bright sunflowers lure you outside to the cottage garden.

The front of the home is comprised of a parlor partially separated from the adjacent dining room by an open squared archway—a slight change to one of the earlier configurations. This offers an open living space that makes the tiny cottage seem larger; it also works better for entertaining. The dining table rests next to a fireplace with a simple unadorned surround, and next to the chimney is a storage cabinet. In keeping with her plans for afternoon teas and entertaining friends, the furniture is clustered so a group of 10–20 can move around the refreshment areas.

A narrow straight-run stairway leads upstairs to two small bedrooms, each with a window under the gables. Since there are few closets and storage areas, DiRicco looked for furniture with drawers and shelves.

The master bedroom has its own bath, and the second bath is off the pantry. Marble sink tops and fixtures for both bathrooms were salvaged from a San Francisco hospital demolition.

To the rear of the porch is the kitchen, an addition dating to 1882 that replaces the original separate summer kitchen. The pantry area offers additional kitchen storage and houses the refrigerator in a convenient location separate from the period kitchen in order not to seem out of place.

On the exterior, DiRicco played detective by scraping the exterior and peeling off layers of paint to discover the original pale yellow hue, which she matched. Similarly, for the interior, she peeled off paint and paper to discover the original surfaces, then contacted specialty stores to either match the original wallpaper or find a close match. Amazingly, the couple discovered all the missing hardware pieces in the garden when they turned the soil.

Advance planning ensures that this cottage will serve as a backdrop for many splendid moments in the future, while the owners are able to connect with the beauty of the past.

above: Storage is always at a premium in a cottage. Here DiRicco filled open shelves with amber glass and other vintage collectibles. Part of the Victorian lifestyle was to prominently and openly display fine items and collections.

left: The sink and drain board were salvaged from a family ranch, along with the bead board, which the couple has fashioned into cupboards.

far left: The original first-growth California redwood slats are visible on the ceiling, corner posts, and one window frame. The single-wall construction has remained intact since the cottage was built almost 140 years ago. The fir floors in the parlor and dining area are original, so they were sanded and refinished. However, in the kitchen and the master bedroom, the floors were bare to the foundation, so maple planks were installed with hopes that the floors would wear and seem original when weathered.

YWCA Cottage
Mill Valley

Mill Valley is a charming village community of 13,600 people nestled in the redwood trees at the southern end of the Marin Peninsula. The small city sits slightly inland from the tip of Richardson Bay, an inlet to the north of the Golden Gate. It is the Golden Gate where the bay meets the ocean and strong currents mix and pull the great waters together. The channel separates the landforms of San Francisco to the south from Mill Valley in Marin County to the north. However, despite this physical separation, the histories of San Francisco and Mill Valley remain closely linked.

The naming of Mill Valley can be traced to the enterprise of the earliest European settler, John Thomas Reed. Reed, an Irish sailor, became a Mexican citizen, married the daughter of the commander of San Francisco's Presidio, and was assigned the first Mexican land grant north of the San Francisco Bay in 1834. According to Mill Valley's Historical Society, Reed built a mill by trading animal skins and hides with the Russians for the mill's necessities.

In 1889, Mill Valley changed from a sleepy town with fewer than 10 lots to 200 lots in one year. When an earthquake and fire devastated San Francisco in April 1906, a number of displaced San Franciscans found refuge in Mill Valley, increasing the population to over 2,500 people. From 1950 to the present, the population has almost doubled.

The cottage tradition in Mill Valley dates back to the time when ferries carried weekenders, vacationers, and campers across the bay. One of these destinations was a YWCA camp that served as a vacation retreat for girls since the beginning of the last century. Very little remained of the camp when successful Marin County entrepreneur Joan Barnes bought two adjacent hillside lots in Mill Valley.

left: This door enters the preserved portion of the YWCA cottage. The walls are board and batten. The painted glass lets in ample light and garden views. The original delightful details of the porch post and corbels were repeated through the expansion.

right: Barnes found this hand-drawn poster dated April 17, 1948, during the remodel. It now hangs in the mudroom.

Barnes found the cottage while house hunting and loved how it sat on the land. While the interior had suffered a number of remodels, she found the exterior profoundly sweet and this became the focus of her new home.

Barnes wanted a home large enough for comfortable family living, and one able to accommodate a home office and a courtyard. She also wanted to retain the unpretentious single-walled board-and-batten cottage with its well-shaped corbels and shaded porch, and to have the new home reflect the integrity of the cottage.

With her clear vision, she organized a trusted team to accomplish expanding the cottage, starting with architect Dirk Stennick of San Francisco. The result is a clustered pavilion of connected cottages that appears to be the whole of the YMCA Camp reclaimed rather than a comfortable new home. It is an example of cottage preservation by incorporating the original 350-square-foot cottage and repeating its forms and materials into the addition. Barnes encourages others who may find a cottage they love, but find it too small, saying, "Preserve it and expand it with extraordinary pizzazz."

above: High bead-board wainscoting runs down this connecting hallway. A lovely hand-painted cupboard accents the entry into the courtyard.

left: The sheltered garden courtyard is Barnes' favorite spot in the morning. An abundance of outdoor art and blooming plants fill the Mediterranean style courtyard. Ceramic containers pick up the courtyard's theme. The kitchen and mudroom on the left are joined to the master bedroom on the right by a breezeway that opens into the courtyard.

right: Informal linens like this vintage tablecloth work well for cottages. They set a tone for casual relaxation.

Like other homes on the winding street, only the garage, a fence, and a gate leading to a downward-sloping stairway can be seen from the road. As you look down from the street, shade trees, fragrant blossoms, and garden art seem more prominent than the home, which from first glance looks like it has been there since the early part of the 20th century. To the left as you descend the stairs sits the original YWCA cottage with its welcoming red front door and overhead transom. When the rebuilding began, this portion enclosed the living room, music room, and a complete kitchen. However, with the redesign, it now encompasses an airy living room and a portion of the dining room.

Renovating the cottage was not a small undertaking. It required a new foundation as well as structural, heating, and electrical work. Even the walls of the original cabin required rebuilding to meet code requirements.

Outside, a new retaining wall supports a level area for a European style courtyard. Throughout the redesign there is a design integrity that belies the expansion. Stennick comments, "Joan Barnes recognized what many others don't—aesthetics are a science, especially when you get into the detail."

To carry out Barnes' vision, the floors and walls are all wood. Painted surfaces were chosen over stained. Painted wood was preferred in selecting furnishings.

Another important consideration in the home's design is the roofline. With the pavilion concept, a variety in the roof angles make the living areas appear to be connected cottages.

above: Art, comfortable furniture, and a piano fill the front parlor. Both the wood-plank floors and walls are cheerfully painted. Walls were removed from the original camp cottage to create this open room. Furnishings feature comfort in unpretentious upholstery and an abundance of throws, pillows, and linens. A similar feeling is obtained in the master bedroom.

left: From the open front door, you can see through the parlor. The size of cottages provides for natural light from as many as three sides.

35

The approach is particularly appropriate for the view looking down from the street entry, as the cluster of roof slopes blends with the rest of the neighborhood yet remains consistent to the cottage concept.

Hallways and breezeways connect the pods of the pavilion. Seizing opportunities for more storage is an understated strong cottage tradition. Barnes then furnished the connecting areas with painted benches, storage cabinets, bookcases, and galleries for books, paintings, and collections.

The geometry that results from piecing the spaces together also better connects the home to the out-of-doors. While not every room enjoys a door to the outside, there is access to the outdoors within a few paces from almost any spot in the home.

Uniting the home with the gardens is another cottage tradition. Because of the area's temperate climate and California's outdoor living traditions, connections to the decks, patios, and courtyards are strong. Courtyards are a living style and tradition inherited from early Spanish designs. The courtyard in this cottage home is perhaps the most beloved space, especially enjoyed early in the day. For watching sunsets, Barnes prefers a second patio that reaches around to the back of the original cottage and connects to the garden by bridged walkways.

above: Bookcases line the hallway leading to the master bedroom. Care in making the hallways a little wider allows for much needed storage.

right: The dining room is a portion of the original YWCA cottage. Note the differences in the board walls. Barnes likes the cottage character of showing how homes grow and change through the years.

above: Freshly cut flowers, fruits, vegetables, and vintage accessories bring life to any cottage kitchen.

left: The white surfaces of the cabinets, tiles, and walls serve as a clean backdrop for a lively room. The center work island is a marble-topped French fish counter with the original graphics retained.

As in many country homes, the kitchen is a central and important room. It has a steeply pitched roof with a skylight that adds to the openness, but the scale of the original YWCA cottage is retained by the low height of the kitchen walls. The central island is the gathering spot during meal preparation. Seating is provided by a cheerful collection of mismatched stools. The cabinets are white with wooden counter-tops that match the salvaged hardwood floors. Walls are white with clean, bright white tiles that give it a homey scrubbed look. The windows are without curtains and look out to the courtyard.

The overall feel of the interior is light, cheerful, and serene. Casual harmony is achieved through the color palette and a scale consistent to the original cottage. The theme of reused and weathered collections repeats for casual informality. A key to this overall effect is the choice of soothing colors for the painted wood. Floors are pale green, gray, or pink with a scattering of vintage rugs. This approach to painting the floors started in the living room and dining room where the cottage floors were stripped to the subfloor planks, then painted pale green. An exception is the kitchen, which has a salvaged, varnished hardwood floor. The dining room has a skylight that illuminates a favorite painting and makes the bench a bright spot to enjoy the sunshine during the day. The bench and the Hoosier-style cupboard feature scraped and weathered paint, suggesting well-loved pieces that have been part of the cottage for a long time. As perfect as most of the furnishings are for the home, most were collected well before Barnes ever found the property.

left: Ample pillows, lush linens, and natural light from all directions mark the bedroom's comfort. Barnes likes the look of oversized furniture in small rooms.

right: Despite its snug size, the bathroom is bright and inviting as a result of the skylight, white paint on the wooden walls, white vintage hexagonal floor tiles, and white shower curtain and towels. The green antique dental cabinet provides storage and is almost a visual pun in the white room.

below: Side-hinged, paned-casement windows are typical for cottages. This bedroom is of entirely new construction, yet carries forth the original cottage's design, scale, and detailing.

Barnes has observed that in the attempt to gain more space, many cottages reclaim outdoor areas. That would mean front porches are enclosed for more space in a living room and outdoor sleeping porches become another room.

The vestiges of incorporating these areas are variations in roof slopes and the appearances inside of wood finishes intended for facing outdoors like board and batten. She likewise used this technique, and an example is the mudroom leading into the kitchen. It features both these aspects, suggesting a progressively expanded home instead of new construction.

Stennick used subtle changes in elevations (slight steps up or down) in the transitions from one living area to another as another technique to suggest a progressively expanded home.

The airy, simple honesty of the original camp cottage continues through the entire home. The overall effect retains the charm of early Mill Valley when campers and weekenders travelled on ferries to escape the bustle of the city.

above: This French daybed is a piece that Barnes purchased specifically for the window-lit corner in the parlor. It is a favorite spot for afternoons with a good book.

right: The enclosed porch that connects to the back patio features a comfortable and inviting built-in window seat.

right: An old birdbath makes a useful planter.

below: A trickling fountain in the courtyard adds a sensory dimension of natural sounds for outdoor relaxation.

Barnes says, "When I come through the gate and walk down the stairs, it is sheltered and protected and delights me to be home." Friends share this sense when they visit. Despite their predisposition to other architecture, including very modern concrete and glass, she says people find themselves comfortable and content in the cottage. Barnes is still discovering the new joys of living in the cottage, "Like the afternoon sunshine flooding into the parlor in the day, the home has a changing life that you sense throughout the day."

During the teardown for construction, Barnes found a camp bulletin board listing flowers that the YWCA girls planted while at camp. She has made a point to plant the same perennial and annual blooms in her garden.

Since Mill Valley enjoys cool summer temperatures and mild winters, Barnes spends much of her time outdoors. The reclaimed brick patio creates a sense of being in the Mediterranean. The qualities of the light are especially wonderful in the morning, and it is a favorite breakfast spot.

Workers' Cottage
Sonoma

Sonoma, a city of less than 10,000 people located north of the San Francisco Bay, carries some impressive distinctions in its history. It was the last of the California missions to be established, and it is known as the birthplace of California's history. Sonoma's first building was a Spanish mission founded in 1823. Mexico took over California from Spain and installed its Governor, Mariano Vallejo, in Sonoma. He took a great interest in the city and in 1834 surveyed the central plaza near the mission, which remains today. On June 14, 1846, a party of Americans from Sutter's Fort (60 miles away in Sacramento) seized Sonoma in the Bear Flag Rebellion, arrested Governor Vallejo, and declared California an independent republic. In July of the same year, California joined the union as a territory. In 1850, it became a state and with statehood, the former Governor Mariano Vallejo became a state senator. Despite Senator Vallejo's efforts, the capitol never returned to Sonoma; and it became a quiet agricultural area rather than the hub of visiting dignitaries that it had been under Mexican rule.

Sonoma remained a somewhat sleepy agricultural town until after World War II, when California's burgeoning wine industry and tourism spurred the economy and expanded the population. Tourists now flock to Sonoma to enjoy wine tasting and to explore the reminders of the area's history. Sonoma State Park has preserved the mission, soldiers' barracks, the square, as well as Governor Vallejo's two homes. The State Park welcomes visitors to tour these buildings.

The Sonoma Chalet is one of the many pleasant places to stay when visiting Sonoma. From the grounds of the inn, you can see and walk to Vallejo's second home, a prefabricated Victorian set amid a vineyard. The Sonoma Chalet began as a working ranch, and Sara's cottage, one of four small cottages on the property, was actually the foreman's home. The larger chalet home was the family home of the Reichmuth family, Swiss hotel owners who moved to Sonoma from San Francisco. The family became active in the community and built a dance hall called Little Switzerland that is still open and popular with locals. The family stopped ranching in the early 1940s, but the buildings that remain on the property provide a reminder of the area's agricultural past.

This tiny workers' cottage provides all of what one might want at the end of a day. The cottage has a simple rectangular shape with a shed roof over an extension to the rear. The exterior walls are comprised of cedar shingles.

In recognition of the Reichmuths, the current owners named the foreman's home Sara's cottage for the wife and mother, and the other three cottages (Laura's, Leslie's, and Sophie's) are named for each of the Reichmuth daughters. The four cottages and rooms in the chalet are available as nightly rentals.

The innkeeper's design approach for the cottages and chalet is to preserve the buildings to the period as much as possible.

above: The kitchen window box overflows with blooms and provides the connection between home and garden that is so much a part of the cottage tradition.

right: The red-cedar paneling and knotty-pine floor are hardy materials which have weathered the time.

left: The porch is ready for enjoying the sunset with local Sonoma favorites—sourdough bread, dried jack cheese, salami, and a bottle of a nearby vineyard's rich red wine.

For Sara's cottage, the inspiration was to return the cottage to the condition that it enjoyed while home to the ranch foreman in the late 1930s and early 1940s. Sara's cottage is a simple rectangular building comprised of less than 600 square feet with a shed roof over an addition in the back and a similar lattice roof over the porch that is supported by simple beams. It is a tidy building, and its simplicity suggests that it may have been constructed with proficient local agricultural labor rather than a professional builder.

Many of California's early cottages, such as this one, were homes for workers. Unfortunately, few of the historic farm, ranch, or railroad cottages remain in an accurate condition to demonstrate as well as this one how working people made their cottages a home.

In the tradition of workers' cottages in the past, this cottage's floor plan is open with a sleeping loft (accessed by a ladder) over the kitchen and bath areas. Rugs and furniture segment the open space into a living-room area and a bedroom.

The owners looked to the last time the cottage was occupied by a ranch foreman for the approach to the furnishings. The walls are the original western red-cedar paneling. Knotty-pine floors are covered with a number of scattered oriental rugs.

above: Sleeping lofts are an easy way to add extra room for overnight guests. It is a cottage style dating back hundreds of years.

right: The floral curtains, sculptural settee, matching chair, and cabinet of favorite books make an evening around the fire seem as a step back in time.

below: The low ceiling of the rear addition is perfectly sized for a bed. Nooks with intimacy of scale help to make living in cottages especially endearing.

The overstuffed furniture pieces create a conversation area around a wood-burning stove. The settee has rounded arms with a tufted decorative pattern in the coral upholstery, very typical of the period. There is a period radio and a collection of classic books, but no television or telephones, transporting visitors back to a quieter, less hectic time. The painted mural near the woodstove is attributed to Alfred Reichmuth, Sara's son and an amateur painter.

The gas stove and adjacent sink and drainboard provide all the essentials for a home-cooked meal, just as they might have done during the early 1940s. The vintage floral drapes, printed linens, and painted furniture take you back to that time. The owners filled the glass-door kitchen cabinet and the built-in floor-to-ceiling hutch with Fiestaware, painted ceramics, and other vintage collectibles.

above: An humble hutch stores and displays the tableware and linens.

right: Floral prints and layered table linens are another cottage style.

left: Bright tiles, floral fabrics, and faux-finished walls add extra interest to the bathroom. This room is spacious enough for a claw-footed tub and a bureau containing bed and bath linens.

right: This lamp reminds visitors of the importance of a good-night kiss. Cottages and romance have long been linked together.

below: Hand-painted tiles are a luxury that becomes affordable in a cottage because so few are needed. Size makes it easier to fill a cottage with the special details that help to make every inch appear well loved while on a budget.

The bathroom is the only room in the cottage with a door. While the ample windows in the bathroom suggest a lack of privacy, to the contrary, the cottage is isolated to the rear of the property, across a footbridge, and amid eucalyptus trees. A dovecote is near enough to hear the soothing cooing inside.

Sonoma is in the heart of California's famous wine country. It is a popular weekend destination for wine-lovers, who tour the area, pause at the tasting rooms, and try new restaurants. Wine grapes were planted at the early missions and popularized in the 1850s by Agoston Haraszthy. Wine became so plentiful by 1911 that firefighters used it to put out a large fire. Now it is rare to see a hillside not covered with vines. This cottage reminds visitors of the important laborers upon whom we depend for raising our food, and of course, wine grapes.

"Green" Bungalow
Palo Alto

Drew Maran's bungalow was built in 1928 on a tree-lined street not far from downtown Palo Alto. This is the same year that Stanford alumnus and benefactor Herbert Hoover was elected President of the United States, amidst great celebrations in Palo Alto. Little is known about the history of the cottage Maran purchased and restored in 1999. However, given the time of its construction, it is possibly linked to someone working at Stanford University.

Don Gaspar de Portola named the area in 1769 after camping beside a tall tree (El Palo Alto) next to the San Francisquito Creek. This same 250-year-old Coastal Redwood still graces the creek and is memorialized as the City of Palo Alto's logo.

Under Mexican rule, the area along the peninsula south of San Francisco was split into a number of land grants and settlers made their living by cattle ranching and farming. This lifestyle began to change in 1863, when the San Francisco and San Jose Railways were completed.

The railroad reduced the travel time for the 35 miles between Palo Alto and San Francisco from a five-hour stagecoach ride to an 80-minute trip by rail. This shorter travel time attracted wealthy San Franciscans to build mansions in nearby Menlo Park.

left: Little besides the absence of curtains suggests the contemporary lines and color inside this cottage on a corner lot not far from downtown Palo Alto.

top right: The "tiled" yard encorporates the building material into the yard while helping maintain the area.

bottom right: A variation in the fence line makes room for two birch trees.

Former Governor Leland Stanford and his wife Jane purchased 740 acres next to Menlo Park and founded Stanford University in 1885; it opened its doors in 1891. Palo Alto incorporated in 1894 as a university town. Growth was slow despite a small influx following the 1906 San Francisco earthquake, and by the 1920's Palo Alto's population reached only 5,900 people. Writer Kathleen Donnelly describes Palo Alto in the 1920s as "a pleasant place full of pleasant homes, many of them owned by Stanford faculty members," adding, "Palo Alto around the '20s didn't actually roar, but they did engage in animated conversation."

Maran's home reflects this modest civility. The two-bedroom cottage home encompasses 960 square feet. Situated on a corner, its tidy exterior suits the neighborhood. There is little automobile traffic but the sidewalk travelers are frequent, providing friendly neighborhood interaction.

Faced with a home and neighborhood deeply rooted to the past, Maran purchased the cottage to be his own residence with the objective of saving it, restoring it, and remodeling it in a way that unites the modern with the past. Key to his approach was remaining true to his personal environmental values. Maran is an active leader for California's "green" building movement. He started his own construction company in 1984 with a clear vision to take a sustainable approach to design, demolition, renovation, and new-home building. He was equally clear about wanting to save the bungalow cottage, saying, "Preservation goes hand in hand with green building." The home's size, age, and construction quality attracted him, as did the neighborhood. The challenges were the low ceilings and the small dark rooms.

Maran completely gutted the house, which allowed for him to create a new floor plan while ensuring structural

above: The hallway provides a view of the lustrous concrete-veneer plastered walls with integrated pigment. The baseboards and door frames are painted cottage-style sparkling white.

left: Clean lines and vibrant colors unite the fireplace and the wall. The custom cabinet houses the media center so the television can be neatly tucked away. The remodeling is reflected in the high ceiling which is not original to the small house.

Dense blooms inside and outside the kitchen window enhance the charming feel of the cottage.

The new floor plan provides an open area flooded by natural light from the skylight that runs on either side of the central beam along the spine. Rugs define the living and dining areas while the kitchen is separated by part of the U-shaped-slate kitchen counter and the cabinets.

integrity and making repairs to damaged wood. With architect Ross Levy of San Francisco and environmental interior designer Sandra Slater of Palo Alto, he redesigned and reconstructed the home with a contemporary vision. On the exterior, little changed. The original roofline was clipped, so Maran extended the eaves to be more consistent with bungalow design. He replaced the roof with salvaged material and reframed the walls with material reclaimed from a movie set. In doing the restoration, he salvaged all the old windows and doors and recycled the demolition waste—both consistent with green-building practices.

On the interior, he saved the Douglas fir floors and reinstalled them, augmenting with other salvaged floor material, when needed. One of the big challenges was to make the interior open and light. The ceilings were opened to the roof for greater height, and Maran installed a long ridge skylight along the sides of the central beam.

Originally, the kitchen, dining room, and living room were separately walled spaces that ran lengthwise down the side of the home, placing the kitchen in the rear. The bedrooms ran down the opposite side of the home. The new floor plan places the kitchen, dining room, and living room in the same open area at the front of the house.

The perforated-metal splashboard follows the soft curve of the counter peninsula and serves as a counterpoint to the square forms of the cabinets on the wall.

French doors with white painted woodwork connect the living room with a deck on the side and provide extra light.

Levy designed a U-shaped counter with a peninsula separating the kitchen from the dining area. The design includes a slight curve to soften the interior to which Slater added a splashboard of perforated metal. Maran says that the balance of mass, the height of the counter, and the proportions of the rooms were main considerations of their renovation planning. Slater and Maran visualized the placement of furniture and planned for circulation well in advance, recognizing that balance and proportion are especially important in small homes such as this cottage.

The stainless-steel bowl of fruit against the white windowsill and frame encapsulates the blending of the old with the new in this cottage remodel.

The warm colors in the walls are integral to the concrete-veneer plaster. This is also part of Maran's approach to green building. The advantages are no off-gassing or need for repainting. The same wall finishes continue throughout the back of the home, which include a master bedroom and bath, and a second bedroom and bath. The home's insulation is blown cellulose that is made from recycled newspapers.

Even the outdoor landscaping was approached sustainably. The exterior decks were made from salvaged redwood, and the redwood in the fence came from certified sustainably managed forests. The concrete contains fly ash (a recycled material.) Some of the outdoor lumber is made from recycled plastic, which is another material that does not require continued painting for upkeep.

Maran thinks his approach to remodeling the bungalow works very well for an urban environment. He says, "It preserves the home while giving it a new identity. Both the preservation and remodel were about conserving resources. Green building is a great tradition for an older home because it is a connection between the thinking of then and now." Maran shares the home with his son. He admits that living in a small space requires thought and planning so that it works for both company and time alone—things like having the television in the living room and the kitchen open to guests. However, he thinks everything about cottage living is terrific—less to maintain, more comfort, and a maximum use of the space and resources.

above: Opaque glass provides privacy for the guest bathroom. While a compact room, the strong horizontal lines of the sleek styling and use of the mirrors give the room a larger presence.

right: With careful planning, the side yard of the corner lot makes useful space for outdoor living. Here the space between the redwood deck and the fence is filled with fast-growing bamboo for a sense of natural shelter.

COTTAGE COMMUNITY
CARMEL-BY-THE-SEA

Carmel-by-the-Sea, or Carmel, is California's much loved and frequently visited cottage community. Splendid natural beauty is the starting point for this mile-square city of less than 5,000 residents who enjoy powdery white sand beaches, the thunderous Pacific Ocean, and groves of rare Monterey pines and cypress. Between Carmel and Pacific Grove winds the famous Seventeen-Mile Scenic Drive.

Carmel retained a quiet existence as a home to fishermen until it attracted the attention of early California land speculators. Santiago Duckworth and his partner, Abbie Hunter, planned a resort to capitalize on the Mission to be linked by a possible extension of the Southern Pacific Railroad line that did not materialize. In 1900, they sold to a real estate salesman from San Jose, James Franklin Devendorf, and his partner Frank Powers. They decided upon an approach to preserve the natural beauty of the area as the focus for their sales efforts. Together they founded the Carmel Development Company promoting "a seaside town on Carmel Beach in the pine forest alongside Carmel Mission."

Devendorf proved to be tireless. He planted trees along Ocean Avenue (now the heart of the business district) and curved roads around trees they encountered while laying out the town. The first brochure targeted educators, and he traveled to Stanford and the University of California at Berkeley to market property for summer homes. Early buyers soon settled on Professors Row, building modest summer cottages and forming discussion and study groups among themselves for lively exchanges. One of the Berkeley buyers was Perry Newberry, who later became Carmel mayor, newspaper publisher, and home builder.

Carmel is only about 130 miles south of San Francisco, and the San Francisco earthquake in 1906 inspired more sales, as did the sale of property to poet George Sterling, a member of San Francisco's Bohemian community, who urged other artists and writers to relocate.

Carmel's arts community is a legend, and includes poet Robinson Jeffers, writer Sinclair Lewis, photographer Edward Weston, painter Xavier Martinez, novelist and essayist Mary Hunter Austin, and journalist Lincoln Steffens. Some of the newcomers moved into old fisherman cottages, while others built new homes that reflected their artistic vision of home.

This 1924 cottage known as Hansel was designed and built by Hugh Comstock to display his wife's dolls. He modeled the 300-square-foot home after an illustration, and this became the first of the Carmel cottages in the storybook tradition. The home appears to be handcrafted with a steep roofline finished with shingles, stone walkways, and a prominent decorative chimney. Comstock named an adjacent cottage, along the same design approach, Gretel.

The Arts and Crafts movement greatly influenced the cottages in philosophy, as William Morris's principles of simplicity, construction by craftsmen rather than by mechanization, and art and architecture in accordance with the nature of materials were embraced by many of Carmel's early residents. A professional class of cottage builders emerged and over time they influenced each other's style and a fanciful Carmel look emerged that is very much reminiscent of the Picturesque cottages of Europe at the end of the 18th century. One important builder was M. J. Murphy, who moved to Carmel in 1904. Another is Hugh Comstock, who, while not an architect, introduced the storybook look when he built the cottage known as Hansel in 1924. The inspiration was an illustration in a children's book. He built the home to appear handcrafted with a steep roofline finished with shingles, a rounded split Dutch door, stone walkways, and a prominent decorative chimney.

With this history, it is not surprising that Carmel remains delightfully unique. Outside the business district there are no sidewalks, only quiet tree-canopied streets. Walking, you notice street names but no addresses. This represents few problems for the post office, because residents congregate at the post office to pick up mail, just as the early writers did in the 1920s. However, other delivery services and emergency services have learned to work with a system of names or a simple identifying description.

The small city has been tightly governed to retain its individuality. The commercial district is laid out with plazas and alleys and retains a mixture of small shops and successful businesses located in converted cottages.

Carmel has continued to be a desirable place to live, and there have been pressures to build larger homes. Some of the new homes reflect cottage designs and materials that try to artfully disguise the larger size.

Members of the Carmel Cottage Society quietly educate others about cottage living. For one of the Society's presentations, long-time Carmel cottage owner Nadya Giusi, wrote a passage that captures the locals' love for their cottages: A cottage is "more than a house, a place to live, or an architectural style. A cottage is a presence with a past, a living entity that will ultimately seduce you into a relationship. What kind of relationship depends on you, but one way or another, a cottage will sneak up on you and grab your heart."

Three Carmel cottage owners have opened their doors to demonstrate their approach to graceful Carmel cottage living: the Pink Cottage, Sticks & Stones, and Murphy Cottage.

Not all newcomers to Carmel are willing to live in a 500–600-square-foot cottage. Some new construction may feature cottage design elements or materials and try to disguise its larger size.

PINK COTTAGE
CARMEL

Pink Cottage, located on Camino Real, the street known as Professors' Row in Carmel, was built in 1927. M. J. Murphy, who had been living and working in Carmel 23 years by that time, designed it. The cottage is sometimes called Celia's Cottage after its original owner, Celia Harris. Harris held degrees as a teacher and a social worker. Part of the Berkeley literaries, she hosted and participated in the Carmel study and discussion groups.

The cottage has a simple single-wall, board-and-batten construction. The material is redwood, and on the interior it has remained lustrous and unpainted. While small and encompassing only two bedrooms, through the years a sloped shed roof was added to house the galley kitchen, and the rooflines show the addition of a breezeway and back bedroom.

The front of the home is balanced and nearly symmetrical with a fireplace in the center of the home on the interior living-room wall.

Pink Cottage has a pure, uncluttered, mostly symmetrical appearance from the street. The garage was added later but repeats the same board-and-batten exterior treatment.

The front door shows more of the Carmel storybook feel. Similar to Hansel, the door is rounded at the top and split into a Dutch door. Another traditional cottage element is the vertically-hinged casement windows.

The current owners, Lois and Jack Prentice, have created a warmly embracing home that fully uses the space without overcrowding it. They are experienced in cottage living, having spent several years in a historic cottage in England.

The pair is active in the Cottage Society. Jack draws ink architectural renderings of various Carmel cottages that are featured monthly in Carmel's local newspaper, *The Pine Cone*. Lois calls cottage living an act of balancing "the charm and the challenges," but if appearances can be trusted, the challenges seem to be well conquered.

The flat deck in the front is a comfortable spot for sitting and visiting with passers-by. Carmel's streets are filled with walkers, runners, and dog-walkers.

top left: Through the top half of the arched Dutch doors, you can see in to the redwood of the single-wall construction. You can also see through the living room to the windows on the other side of the home. Because of their size, cottages enjoy natural light from multiple sides.

bottom left: Artisan-crafted objects such as this doorbell add to the home's individual character.

right: Containers of blooming plants next to the Dutch doors welcome visitors. Ceramics and sculpture accent walkways, courtyards, and the garden.

above: The vertically-hinged casement windows are a cottage tradition popular in Craftsman homes. The unpainted woodwork and visible beams may also be a result of Craftsman influences. The Arts and Crafts movement was philosophically embraced by many in the art an academic communities at the time.

right: A breezeway leads to the back bedroom that is wide enough for a daybed and a bureau. The addition to this cottage, like many others, marks a change in roof slopes, adding to the cottage's personality.

The long galley kitchen uses the space as efficiently as any ship. In the kitchen design, they have kept to the same light green hue, including adding a decorative panel to the refrigerator. This is a technique used by other cottagers, where the homogeneity of color unifies the space and gives it a larger, less confining appearance. Another cottage technique is the series of narrow open shelves, where Lois displays her china.

Where the dining area starts, the Prentices placed an antique wooden Scottish Mill cabinet that exactly fits the space as a sideboard. They enjoy hosting holiday dinners, and expand the dining table out in the courtyard where they can seat a crowd. Like the kitchen, the living- and bedrooms' nooks and crannies are filled with shelves for books and ornaments from their travels.

above: The passageway to the front bedroom provides space for shelves with mementos, the things the owners collect that happily remind them of other times and other places.

left: The sideboard is a cabinet from a Scottish mill. It slides into the space as efficiently as a built-in.

far left: The narrow kitchen fits into a shed-roof addition. It is as space-efficient as a galley on a ship.

The courtyard celebrates Carmel's mild Mediterranean climate. French doors open into the courtyard from the main living area. A door to it from the bedroom and the bedroom's large paned windows access every breeze. The courtyard provides plentiful space for entertaining guests. The Prentices will even move the dining-room table outside and add all of the table's leaves to host a large group for Thanksgiving, and Lois notes the weather has always cooperated.

above: The Prentices make ample use of containers in the courtyard so that the greenery can be enjoyed from within the home.

left: The outdoor courtyard is an extension of the living area and transitions the home to the garden setting. Because of most of California's temperate climate, courtyards are part of the California cottage style.

right: Jack's art pieces are sprinkled throughout the garden. The glorious Carmel climate makes gardening possible year-round.

STICKS & STONES
CARMEL

For forty years, Sticks & Stones, built in 1925, has been home to artist and teacher Joe Tanous and his wife, Louise, a doctorate anthropologist and teacher. Both are active in the community after retiring as educators. Joe exhibits his paintings, sculptures, and ceramics in local galleries, and Louise volunteers time for community organizations. The builder, Perry Newberry, who was early mayor and community leader, built 14 different cottages in his career. It was his custom to move into the home he just completed and to start another, selling the one he was living in after the new home was completed.

The home's exterior walls are finished with granite boulders, said to be the last quarried stones from the site of the Carmelite monastery. The small home sits on two city lots, surrounded by lush plantings, and the home wraps around three sides of a central courtyard. The courtyard is set with large tables for enjoyable outdoor family dinners.

above: The gate carries the cottage's name Sticks & Stones. In Carmel, no other address is needed.

79

Originally the cottage was comprised of one bedroom, and a previous owner added a second. To accommodate their family, Joe and Louise added a dining room and a guest house in the back, and connected the new portions with additional walkways and garden courtyards. The real changes have been to the surrounding neighborhood. The homes surrounding Sticks & Stones are newer, larger, and serve as vacation homes. While it makes for a quiet neighborhood, since it is seldom that anyone is home, it certainly cuts down on the neighborly chatter over the fence and the exchange of garden vegetables that Newberry probably envisioned.

above: The granite chimney is prominent on the front of the home. One path leads to the back courtyard at the center of the U-shaped home; the other takes guests to the main entrance.

left: With the top half of the Dutch doors open, you can see through the living room to the windows on the other side.

right: Containers of geraniums next to the Dutch doors welcome visitors. Ceramics and sculpture accent walkways, courtyards, and the garden.

81

Inside the home, the Tanous's collections, like copper utensils, fill the cottage. Louise is interested in household objects and also collects wooden potato mashers and wooden wine stoppers, along with Somoan carvings and South Pacific artifacts.

above: Joe Tanous mixes his own sculture with found objects and displays them in the garden.

right: Door-to-door is the look from the dining room through the collection of copper utensils to the kitchen and the second Dutch door.

With the exception of some of the dining-room additions, the board-and-batten walls, ceiling, and exposed beams on the interior are painted white. The light reflecting from the many doors and windows give it a cheerful brightness, and the white backdrop serves to set off the interesting artwork and collections.

Joe's paintings and sculptures fill the home alongside of other artworks that he has collected. Collecting is an interest the couple shares.

The builder of the home, Perry Newberry, was one of Carmel's earliest residents. He was an outspoken mayor, and published Carmel's newspaper, *The Pine Cone*. Poet Robinson Jeffers credited Newberry's influence for keeping Carmel quiet and protecting its trees.

above: In the home, they display collections of wooden potato mashers. Both enjoy making discoveries at yard sales.

left: The vaulted ceiling is open to the support beams, adding height and airiness. The paintings were done by Tanous.

right: The drop in the ceiling provides a perfect nook for the grand piano. The pieces beneath the gable are Polynesian boat carvings that interest anthropologist Louise.

FAIRY-TALE MURPHY
CARMEL

Bob and Mary Condry's cottage north of the business district in Carmel is one that does not have a name, but it carries an interesting history. First occupied in 1936 or 1937, it was designed by M. J. Murphy, the same man who built Pink Cottage ten years earlier. In its materials, design, and detailing, it shows the progression of the storybook influence introduced by Hugh Comstock.

The cottage was originally about 600 square feet and constructed of stucco, stone, and wood. The styling is more similar to Hansel than to the more Craftsman-appearing Pink Cottage. The home is asymmetrical, with a prominent Carmel stone chimney at the side. There are two gables, one facing the front. Decorative bargeboards finish the front gable, and similar handcrafted, painted boards whimsically outline the front door and the windows. The cedar-shingled roof is textured, as is the roughly applied stucco.

The split Dutch door in front is similar to that of the Pink Cottage. The shaded path and courtyard are stone, and the blooming cottage garden has a number of near-secret spots with benches and chairs to sit on.

The light green stucco and wood trim of the Murphy-designed storybook cottage nestles in and blends with the cottage garden. Built ten years after Pink Cottage, it shows a progression toward the styling introduced by Comstock.

above: The shaded front courtyard is made an inviting place to sit with the addition of a small table and containers of blooming plants amidst the foliage of the cottage garden.

left: The Condrys have lushly planted the side of the home to provide beautiful garden views to enjoy through the windows or when sitting outdoors.

right: Carmel's Mediterranean climate invites you outside for gardening, reading, relaxation, or wonderful walks.

88

Inside are open-beamed ceilings and a split-run stairway to a loft. The stairs are so steep that you have to back down carefully. The Condrys took advantage of the area beneath the stairs for additional storage. The interior doors and woodwork show remarkable craftsmanship. Bob Condry mentioned that many ship carpenters worked in the Carmel area, and this would explain the trim and exact woodwork. The floors are oak. The walls and ceiling are painted white, and the Condrys decorated with wicker furniture for a casual garden look. They also used the same color palette to make the spaces feel larger and connected.

While oversized upholstered pieces add to comfort, the Condrys resisted and instead selected wicker. The furnishings on the interior fit the scale of the cottage. The extensive back patio is also filled with wicker furniture.

above: An inserted window box in the bathroom provides a convenient ledge for plants that bring the garden indoors.

left: The vaulted ceiling and light color open up the small space. The plank door that opens to the kitchen features hand-forged hinges. These and the hand-sawn balusters suggest a ship's carpenter may have worked on the interior.

right: Hand-painted flowers around the recessed alcove with shelves in the diminutive bathroom demonstrate how touches of creativity turn the ordinary into the extraordinary.

One of the careful additions is an enclosed sunporch on the back of the home. Mary has furnished it with a daybed filled with fanciful pillows. From here, you can look out to the ocean and enjoy the outdoors no matter what the weather. A deck out to the back also shares these views and provides a roomy space for outdoor entertaining.

above: You can peak into the dayroom from the large deck. Both enjoy spectacular views to the ocean.

right: An enclosed porch reclaims living space and adds a delightful corner for looking outside or enjoying a cup of tea and a good book.

FOREST COTTAGES
TAHOE

In the high rugged Sierras just south of Donner Pass, lie the blue waters of the third deepest lake in North America, Lake Tahoe. This natural lake reaches a depth of 1,685 feet, so deep that it doesn't freeze in winter. Lake Tahoe is nicknamed "Lake in the Sky," a term used by early explorers. Before that the Washoe Indians called it "Big Waters," and big it is. The lake stretches 22 miles long and 12 miles wide with a third of it falling in California's neighboring state of Nevada in an alpine environment at 6,235 feet in elevation.

Explorer and surveyor John C. Fremont's party, led by Kit Carson, came upon the Lake in the Sky in 1844. Settlers were attracted to the area for cattle grazing and timber harvesting. The surrounding forest hosts Incense cedar, Douglas fir, Mountain hemlock, white fir, and eight species of pine. When Nevada's Comstock Lode was discovered, attention again turned to Tahoe's forests for fuel material and lumber to shore the mines beneath Virginia City. Fortunately for the forest, the silver was exhausted before the trees, leaving Tahoe scenic.

In the 1900s, Tahoe became a retreat for the wealthy. They traveled by train (the original Central Pacific tracks) to Truckee, then switched to a narrow-gauge railroad that ran from Truckee to the lake. From there, travelers went by boats to elaborate vacation homes.

Between 1920 and 1930, the completion of roads to Lake Tahoe meant people of more modest means could rent cottages during the summer and enjoy the pleasures of a lakeside resort.

The brickwork demonstrates a traditional style of regular brick quoins (the corner work) and doorframe, while the remaining bricks are set in a joyful random pattern called "tumbling in." The decoratively sawn bargeboards along the eaves provide additional ornamentation.

95

This river-rock cottage revives the tradition of stone cottages in areas with little timber but good stone quarries. Note the corners are stones cut for regularity and strength.

The Cottage Inn is a remnant of those 1930 summer resorts. Located in California's Tahoe City on the west side of the lake, it is tucked among a community of private cottages next to a sandy beach peppered with pines. Many of these homes reflect traditional lakeside cottage styling with painted clapboard siding, white trim, and paned glass. Other cottages, as well as the Cottage Inn reflect the Tahoe cottage style, a unique blending of lakeside cottage detailing and cabin materials like knotty-pine paneling and floors. The choice of logs and timber is hardly surprising, given the abundance of forest, but the cottage styling tells the story of Tahoe's history as a popular summer resort. It was not until the 1950s that snow removal enabled people to recreate during the winter to make Lake Tahoe a year-round resort.

The Pomin family built the Cottage Inn in 1938. At that time, families would rent a cottage for the entire summer, rather than for the night as is common today. The cottages are placed in a semicircle around a large lawn. Inside, each is differently appointed and the names reflect the interior accents. The exteriors similarly vary while retaining traditional cottage detailing like rounded eyebrows in the shingled roof, stone quoins on the corners, ornamental fireplaces, and roomy front porches. Conversions have eliminated some, but not all, of the original kitchen units. Many cottages retain shared walls, an old tradition common with the workers' cottages of the 17th and 18th centuries.

Lakes, beaches, and cool summer temperatures provide relief for visitors from California's hot interior valleys. There remain plenty of diversions like hiking, camping, boating, fishing, alpine skiing, Nordic skiing, gambling at the Nevada casinos, and exploring the history of Tahoe. While much of the new construction embraces lodge and cabin traditions, a sharp eye can spot the influence of the summer cottages built with mountain materials.

The distinction between cabins and cottages is a narrow one. However, in the cluster of very individual cottages, each displays evidence of cottage traditions.

The vertical positioning of the logs give this cottage a fresh look. The rounded patterns in the shingled roof are called eyebrows, an application that demonstrates immense skill. The eyebrows give an impression of earlier thatched and tiled cottage roofs.

The "Bit of Bavaria Cottage" departs from English traditions and builds upon the styles of similarly forested and snowy Bavaria. This two-story unit, offers breathtaking views through the treetops to the lake and mountains. It is perfectly placed for being snowed in and catching up on novels or knitting.

above: Small details matter. Knotty-pine paneling, carved and painted flowers on the chairs, and diamond-paned windows add simple cottage cheer to the kitchen table area.

right: The frangrance of a spicy coffee cake just out of the oven fills the "Bit of Bavaria" cottage.

left: In small open cottage spaces, you can view the rooms together. Recognizing that, this cottage repeats the same print fabrics in the drapes, valances, and chair upholstery of adjoining rooms. The pillows and throws soften the room's feel, counteracting the sharp corners and the roughness of the stonework.

The detailing in the Bavarian style cottage is ever conscious of size and intimacy. As an example, the stenciling fills but does not crowd the curtain box, the panel in front of the sink, and the decoratively sawn board above the range.

Cottage spaces demand detailing like this and serve as an interesting contrast to modern architecture where the overall volumes of space and movement of light take center stage and decorative touches detract from this design and seem fussy. Cottage spaces crave this kind of fuss.

above: The decoratively sawn and stenciled board trim projects an alpine feel. The stenciled pattern repeats throughout the room.

left: The slope of the roof created an area where the ceiling height is too low to stand, yet allows an opportunity for a built-in desk ornamented by hand-stenciling.

right: Every inch counts in this cheery kitchen. The low eave space houses a workspace and stovetop with room for a half refrigerator, a microwave, and a cabinet below.

above: The spiral staircase that leads to an upstairs sleeping loft takes less space than conventional stairs and the style dates back to those popular in early cottages.

right: The corner behind the spiral stairs provides space for a table. Space is at a premium in this 400–500-square-foot home.

102

The Cottage Inn demonstrates how to follow a basic design theme and to add variations to it. In this case, the cottages share an overall look of natural unpainted wood and knotty-pine accents. However, for each guest suite, there is a design theme that is developed by the use of fabrics, rugs, artwork, and accents.

The Tahoe cottages are named to reflect their own particular design theme. Some examples of these themes are "The Old Fishin' Hole," "Tahoe Tepee," and "Skier's Chalet." This is a natural design approach for collectors.

For the fishing-hole theme, there are creels, bamboo rods, and mounted and framed hand-tied flies. The tepee theme invites searching for and displaying trading post goods, piling on blankets, and framing beadwork. The skiing theme makes great use of old skis and poles and by digging deep into a good junk store, you can find black-and-white photographs of skiers and ski schools from many years ago.

above: The rough willow furniture and timbers demonstrate the merging of cabin materials and cottage design that make the Tahoe cottage style. The porch for the Hunter's Lodge cottage continues a rustic-and-rugged theme while remaining mindful of comfort.

left: The extremely compact bathroom of the Hunter's Lodge cottage makes use of all possible space. The black-and-red flannel shower curtain and knotty-pine paneling add to the woodsy feel.

103

Vernacular Cottage
Hollywood

Early cottages were vernacular, meaning they were built by people for themselves according to familiar traditions and with available materials. Husband and wife artists Daniel Gonzales and Janet Stengo added the extra ingredient of expressing their personal philosophies when they created their backyard cottage in North Hollywood.

Hollywood is a city built more upon illusion than genuine deeply held belief systems. Like much of Southern California, Hollywood was first an agricultural area where the climate supported crops like hay, grain, bananas, and pineapples. Development pressures hit early, and by 1886, the land was subdivided and sold to Midwesterners as winter residences.

By 1903, Hollywood incorporated as a separate city; however, when water supplies fell short, it annexed to adjacent Los Angeles. Eight years later, the Nestor Film Company moved into the old Blondeau Tavern on Sunset Boulevard and started producing westerns and comedies. Other film companies moved west to Hollywood for the year-round climate. The film industry soon dominated the economy and neighborhoods rose up to meet the needs of the many employees and support businesses for the mammoth movie studios.

The Stengo/Gonzales's 1926 home dates to the era of rapid Hollywood expansion. It is in a quiet neighborhood with busy sidewalk interaction between neighbors. Like some of the other homes in the neighborhood, it is stucco with a red-tiled roof. A part of the roof is flat, but the portion over the living room is gabled with a moderate slope. Perhaps it is Spanish Colonial Revival or Mission Revival, or a mingling of the two styles.

The traditional exterior of the 1926 home belies the colorful surprises inside and the garage-to-cottage conversion behind the home.

The original home was comprised of only two bedrooms, but an earlier home owner added a third. It is a home with considerable charm in its detailing. The living room has a rounded barrel ceiling and a stylish fireplace. The coved ceiling in the dining room is also quite unique.

With two teenagers at home, the couple needed more space. Gonzales looked to the garage. It was redwood and stucco with a flat roof and a dirt floor, and the doors were too small to allow passage of today's cars. He, however, saw beauty and potential.

The inspirations for remodeling the garage came from the original California missions founded by Junipero Serra in the 18th century when California was still under Spanish rule. The couple embarked upon a grand tour and returned full of design images.

above: Blue and gold painted trims make the arched entry to the living room from the dining room in the main house anything but ordinary.

right: The barrel ceiling and angular fireplace were the starting points for this room's décor. The owners continued this décor with saturated colors, dramatic lighting, and the artists' handmade furniture pieces.

far right: Paint, stenciling, and shelves for collectibles make for a colorful, zesty kitchen in the main house.

Stengo and Gonzales call their cottage creation "folk architecture," which they define as transforming ordinary environments into beautiful living spaces. They are inspired by the great builders of the world, from indigenous peoples to classic cultures. They undertook their designs with a belief that environments have a direct influence on spiritual consciousness.

For materials, they sought to recycle and reuse. Their sources were the local building-material recyclery, friends, yard sales, and thrift stores. In our complex and affluent society, perhaps these have replaced the readily available natural materials that early cottagers gathered for constructing their homes. Gonzales estimates they spent about $10,000 on the backyard garage-to-cottage conversion, and more than half of this was spent on electrical, plumbing, and carpentry supplies.

The mission design influence is obvious from the front facade. The curving and arching parapet holds a bell. The walls are mud, and the wooden posts that support the roof project through to the front exterior. Other influences are the colors, statuary alcoves, and courtyard garden. The couple reused the redwood garage doors to make the wainscoting, and salvaged and reinforced large panes of office glass with intact mullions and muntins. From these, Gonzales made windows, French doors, and sliding doors.

The French doors open into the main living space with a convenience kitchen for guests. The lustrous floor has a mandala pattern made from cast-off polished granite remnants. Salvaged shutters make up the shelf doors above the counter. The claw-foot tub in the bathroom was a gift from a friend. The temple-style doorway leading to the bedroom/meditation room is split in the center, a technique useful for small spaces because the opened doors interfere less in the room. The bedroom/meditation room leads to Janice's secret garden at the rear of the cottage.

The main house enjoys the same saturated colors and carefully painted detailing. Gonzales's functional art pieces grace both this home and the cottage. The original home and the cottage are united by courtyards and landscaping with accents of painted furniture, collectibles, and garden art that are as original and inspired as the folk architecture of the cottage. The space outside the master bedroom is semienclosed to resemble a Vietnamese river hut, but instead of a river, it sits alongside of the hot tub and pool. There is a side courtyard by the door leading to the kitchen, which connects to the larger courtyard in front of the mission cottage.

above: The old Wedgwood range and paned glass bring an inside look to the outside courtyard.

far left: Looking down the side yard to the back there is another courtyard along with a Mission-influenced guest cottage complete with bell tower. Stengo and Gonzales began the design process with a tour of the California missions. The cottage courtyard is a favorite place for neighbors and friends to gather and be serenaded by Gonzales on the guitar.

Off the main home's master bedroom and next to the hot tub, Stengo and Gonzales partitioned off a section to resemble a Vietnamese river hut. Surrounded with candles, containers of plants, and garden art, the hot tub spills over into the swimming pool.

All combine to create an individual and very rich environment that could never be suspected from the conservative face of the house. Could Hollywood have made a more magical transformation? Mission accomplished.

top left: The home owners pieced together polished granite remainders to create the mandala pattern in the guest cottage floor.

top right: The design and color of the statuary alcove in the back cottage were inspired by the couple's tour of the California missions—the initial inspiration for the garage-to-cottage conversion.

left: The mission detailing is apparent in the ceiling, statuary alcoves, and the style of the wooden window molding.

left: The bathroom's rounded door frame is part of the mission styling. The clawfoot bathtub is a treasured gift from a friend. The hinged-casement windows open to Janice's secret garden and bring the freshness of the flowers into the room.

right: Gonzales turned salvaged windows into sliding doors. This door leads from the cottage meditation room to the bamboo-lined secret garden.

left: The original driveway was converted into a courtyard located between the main house and the back cottage. Narrow side yards are a troublesome area for most home owners to landscape or even to be useful for other than a passageway. Stengo and Gonzales turned theirs into another courtyard that can be separated from the cottage courtyard by bamboo gates that they made.

below: The handmade ladder continues the Mission theme, but to the rear on this side of the cottage, Janice requested a storybook split Dutch door to access the garden and pool from the bedroom. Wire secures potted geraniums to the ladder. The set of laughing figures on the bench were yard-sale finds.

above: Inside the hand-made zigzagged window frame, Gonzales painted the glass and the hinged on the panels. The hanging African inspired art piece to the right was done by one of the owners of Gypsy Wheel.

CROWN OF THE VALLEY
PASADENA

Pasadena was a nameless, quiet, cattle-raising and farming area, from the founding of the nearby Mission San Gabriel Archangel and the establishment of ranches at the turn of the 19th Century. Then, in 1873, a group from Indiana was inspired to escape the harsh winters and to try their hand at raising citrus and fruit, and the San Gabriel Orange Grove Association was born. A community of fewer than 400 "orchardists" lived in the area until a real estate boom in 1885. They met and named the city Pasadena after a Chippewa (not at all native to the area) word said to mean Crown of the Valley. The agricultural economy was soon replaced by tourism with the completion of the Southern Pacific and Santa Fe railroads and the development of large luxurious hotels. By the turn of the 20th century, it had fully evolved into a fashionable winter resort. Wealthy visitors built winter homes and others established themselves as permanent residents.

Pasadena quickly became a lively social and cultural community, hosting the first Tournament of the Roses Parade on January 1, 1890. Trolleys crossed the community, and the Mr. Lowe Railway cable car carried visitors up the mountain. In the 1890s, Cal Tech was founded as a small academic and technical school and it progressed by the 1920s to become a premier science institution. Its graduating students provided a skilled workforce for the Jet Propulsion Laboratory, still an important employer. In 1905, the Mt. Wilson

Observatory was built, and in 1917 a community theater was founded, the famous Pasadena Playhouse.

Pasadena's architecture reflects this history and the abundance of the affluence of its early residents. Orange Grove Boulevard was lined with grand Victorians and boasted 15 millionaire residents. The civic center is hailed as one of the great

above: A lustrous amethyst-hued Craftsman lamp with an art-glass shade and the marginal patterns of the window glass stress the importance of hand-detailing during the Craftsman period.

left: The home owners have furnished the bungalow to the period. The handsome chair was made by Lifetime.

successes of the City Beautiful Movement and the major buildings were designed by some of the period's most well-known national architects.

Perhaps Pasadena's most famous resident architects were brothers Charles Sumner Greene and Henry Matthew Greene. Their firm, Greene and Greene, produced domestic architecture in the Craftsman style that came to the United States from England primarily by Gustav Stickley.

In contrast to the Victorian styles, Craftsman homes were woodsy, connected to the ground and the gardens, and featured the natural colors of the materials. Architectural historians call out Swiss Chalet, Tudor, and Oriental influences in its forms, but the intellectual derivation is from England. It traces first to the Garden City Movement, an effort inspired by Pugen, Ruskin, and Morris to capture the wholeness of preindustrialized life in England, and Freestyle, which blended folk and medieval strains in an attempt to create simplicity and orderliness in a modest cottage.

Smaller Craftsman homes were called bungalows, a word derived from Hindu for a Bengali, a temporary single-story dwelling with a thatched roof. Pasadena and Berkeley are home to the largest numbers of bungalows in California. In Pasadena, a neighborhood rich with bungalows formed a Landmark District that protects the appearance of the homes. Nicknamed "Bungalow Heaven," the neighborhood opens its doors each spring for a tour to educate and share the particular aesthetics and style of bungalow living. Two homes from this neighborhood opened their doors for photographs. As a counterpoint, a vacation cottage is featured that is designed by Frank Lloyd Wright.

Heavenly Bungalow
Pasadena

Craftsman bungalows were intended to be the ideal place to raise a family amid the beauty of natural materials, handcrafted details and a surrounding garden. When bungalows became popular in the United States, the Victorian period was coming to an end.

Some see the popularity of bungalows as a reaction to the formality, ornamentation, social pretentiousness, and vertical style of the Victorians. According to the research of the Bungalow Heaven home owners, the bungalow was a practical choice for families at the time they were built. They were well-suited to a warm climate with verandas for sitting outdoors, overhanging eaves protecting the windows from direct sun, and multiple windows providing cross-ventilation to cool rooms before air conditioning. Some were individually designed by architects, while others were designed by builders inspired by pattern books. It was even possible to buy a prefabricated bungalow in a kit.

Martin Ratliff and Carol Polanskey found a delightful home in Bungalow Heaven. It had fortuitously had its original woodwork and floor plan preserved. According to the couple, builder John K. Johnson constructed their home in 1909 along with others in the neighborhood. Initially, Ratliff/Polanskey removed old carpet and the bars from the windows, and undertook some large improvements to structurally prepare the home to withstand the jars from the earthquakes that sometime shake

This Craftsman bungalow is a celebration of materials and workmanship. The exterior is painted clapboard with decorative mustard-colored bargeboards on the front house and porch gables. The tails of the bargeboards are intricately sawn. The stone porch supports incorporate clinker brick, a popular Craftsman material.

Pasadena. However, they were delighted with the original crafted details like the oak floors, artistic Craftsman window glass, built-in bookcases, a shapely half-course angled staircase, and pocket doors between the living and dining rooms.

Despite these many features, it was the original built-in dish-display case in the dining room that completely won Polanskey over. The clear, leaded art glass had an ornate floral pattern nontypical in Craftsman houses, but more consistent with some of the Art Nouveau designs of the same period.

They moved cautiously before making any changes, careful to research the original condition of the home. Both felt that it was impossible to improve upon the original design, so instead they sought to restore it. When asked about the storage needs for a contemporary family living in a small 100-year-old home, Polanskey, a scientist, shrugged off the problem. "It's true that the amount of things we had didn't correspond to the available storage, but I felt that the problem was that I packed around far more than we really need," she explained. "I simply got rid of things. Our storage is now adequate and I don't miss a thing."

They have furnished and decorated the home to correspond to the period. The matched living-room furniture is by Lifetime, a contemporary furniture maker to Stickley, which made the dining-room table. The subtle dining-room wallpaper is a hand-printed edition of a period design. The original hardwood floors are oak, but the remainder of the interior woodwork, including the front door, is Douglas fir. The two wooden rails in the living and dining rooms are picture rails (the highest) for hanging artwork, and the lower is a plate rail for ceramic display. The home is unusual in that the first home owner decided against building a fireplace, opting instead for more windows.

A built-in bookcase separates the living room from the front entry. This technique separates function while keeping the floor plan open for natural light and air circulation. Lustrous Douglas fir was used to construct the built-in bench, wainscoting, and sideboard. The transom window is a vestige from when the service porch behind was open to the outdoors. It has since been enclosed.

Martin selected the three colors for the exterior paint after researching bungalows throughout the area. His selections have so impressed others that strangers come to the door asking for the name and maker of the colors. Their next challenge was to paint the white living-room walls with period colors and to restore the kitchen.

The woodwork and light fixtures are all original. On the far wall, the original home owner opted for the large middle window instead of a fireplace, which would be more typical. Hidden pocket doors can be drawn to close off the dining room, but remain open most times to make the home feel larger and less segmented.

This typically craftsman dining room makes a transition from the Victorian designs that aimed to impress to a more informal and honest approach. The wooden picture rail, the horizontal windows, and the wainscoating all help anchor the room lower.

Sitting at the table, decorative elements are at eye level. Consistent with the craftsman philosophy, the result is a feeling of simplicity and orderliness. There are natural finishes to the materials. This increases an awareness of the materials' natural properties. The low scale celebrates the importance of people.

Handiwork and craftsmanship are readily evident in the built-in storage units.

above: The Arts and Crafts movement disdained industrial production that replaced handcrafted with machine-made goods. The many subtle variations in this sideboard show it has been lovingly fashioned by hand.

left: The beautiful clear leaded glass in the built-in sideboard convinced Polanskey that they should buy the home. The lovely floral pattern is atypical for Craftsman homes; glass patterns were usually more geometric.

RESTORED CRAFTSMAN
PASADENA

When Manish Raval first saw his home, it completely captivated him with its compact charm. In a neighborhood of horizontal Craftsman lines and homes nested deep into the site and landscape, the cluster of little domed-porch homes on Claremont Avenue in Bungalow Heaven stands out. They are unusual in their small size (675 square feet before any additions) and equally diminutive lots and by their delicate porch posts and vertical reach. It is almost as though the builder could not quite let go of a happy memory centered on a Queen Anne Victorian porch.

Raval's 1922 cottage was not always so pleasantly cheerful and fresh. Its previous owner, Jan Ledgard, slowly recovered this engaging charm piece by piece over three years, and had only finished it three days before Manish found and bought it.

By the time Ledgard bought it, it had sat neglected and disfigured by careless remodeling. A kitchen and bathroom designer by profession, Ledgard undertook to rebuild the home with her own labor. It was unliveable, so on her first day of ownership, she brought in a dump truck and tore apart the inside, outside, and the landscaping. She rebuilt starting with electrical, plumbing, and replastering. Traces of the original construction, the surrounding homes in Bungalow Heaven, and her own memories of cottages in her native Yorkshire guided her efforts. She restored the original porch, the one-bedroom

This cottage squeezes between two large corner lots. The low wall is part of the Yorkshire influence in the remodel. However, instead of topping it with a small picket fence, Ledgard sowed rows of tall blooming plants. A previous owner had enclosed the porch for another bedroom. Ledgard restored it when she overhauled the house with the goal of making it "imperfectly perfect" like the cottages in her native Yorkshire.

The hardwood floors and the wooden fireplace surround and mantel are original. The Craftsman windows brightly light the living room. The owner has chosen a contemporary minimal look for the furnishings, which complements rather than overwhelms the architectural detailing.

floor plan, the fireplace, along with the dining-room and hallway cabinets.

The goal was an overall feeling from the typical cottages of the English countryside, a feeling she describes as, "untidy tidiness," and "imperfectly perfect"—sort of an English *wabi-sabi*. She replicated the original glass with a Craftsman pattern, now available as Showcase, that features marginal lights (the technical term for a panel of glass.) The woodwork was Craftsman in style, but as she investigated, she found that it had always been painted. In keeping, she painted it with white paint softened by hints of color. She painted the walls various hues of yellow, and calls this out as a tip for cottages and small spaces: maintain the same color scheme to make the space feel more unified and larger, but change the value of the color in different rooms for interest. In a few instances, Ledgard relied upon the store of salvaged material by other residents of Bungalow Heaven for things like replacing closet doors.

For the kitchen, she chose a Shaker look for the cabinets and incorporated built-in appliances for a smooth, uninterrupted appearance and maximum storage and work space. She made two

Ledgard stripped off a dark lacquered finish that had been applied to the mantel and surround. She also hand-cut the earth-toned tiles to create the diamond patterns.

choices contradicting the Craftsman tradition that she felt were well justified. One was the selection of maple for its rich glow for the cabinets instead of traditional oak or cherry. The second decision was to install a window box. She pursued this design because the angled beveled glass provides maximum natural light and the protruding shelf offers a place for plants and personal items so that it feels homier. The counter tile is repeated in the floor, a common treatment from the 1920s.

Raval is still working on furnishing his new cottage, but his choices have built upon a look of light, uncluttered, contemporary airiness, with cheerful colors. A low wall protects the garden. In Yorkshire, this would usually be topped by a picket fence; but for now, the yard is screened by blooming plants. This makes the unusual round-domed porch a favorite place for quiet relaxation and interacting with the friendly neighbors in Bungalow Heaven, where everyone seems to know the name of everyone else's dog.

left: As a result of careful space planning and choosing consistent colors and materials, the small walk-through kitchen becomes highly functional with simple, graceful lines.

above: The Craftsman style bookcases are original. While the woodwork in most Craftsman homes was left unpainted to showcase the beauty of the material, research indicated the wood in this home had always been painted.

La Miniatura
Pasadena

Toward the end of Pasadena's bungalow- and cottage-building boom in 1923, the famous American architect, Frank Lloyd Wright, created his own idea of a cottage. Commissioned by a former client from the Midwest, Alice Millard, he designed "the little studio house" that he later named La Miniatura. Built out of a then new material, concrete block (a material he called "that despised outcast") his version of the cottage studio for Millard illustrates Wright's vision that America needed its own style of architecture. Even with this shift in design, he remained true to many ideals of a cottage style.

Wright wrote, "Concrete is a plastic material susceptible to the impressions of the imagination." Because of its design, scale, siting, and landscaping, La Miniatura is by far the most romantic of the block houses he designed in the Los Angeles area in the '20s. The cottage is built on a ravine and consists of three stories.

top left: The patterned block is made with sand from the site. It gives texture and rhythm to the walls. Here the entry courtyard has a planter and the perforated blocks have glass inserted for daylight to spill into the entry.

bottom left: The glass and redwood doors are low to compress the scale, offering an immediate feeling of protective shelter.

far left: The entry to the home is off a courtyard on a small side street. The second- and third-story bedrooms are visible through the narrow windows that look out onto a wooded ravine.

131

The main level is accessed from the street. Wright often compressed the scale of the entry to create a dramatic contrast to the soaring ceiling height in the main room, and this is the experience upon entering La Miniatura, as the ceiling quickly becomes two stories. The soaring space has tall, full doors and windows. Doors open to a balcony that overlooks the gardens and pond, and all combine to give the impression of much greater space than actually exists.

The downstairs has tall, narrow redwood-framed windows and doors that open onto a patio and access the reflecting pond with stepping stones. On this level also are a small kitchen, dining area, and a small maid's room. A sleeping porch and artist's studio are on the upper level, and on the main floor beneath is the master bedroom.

Wright believed that by using concrete block, a product he called the cheapest and ugliest thing in the building world, he could transform the material and design a small cottage home to fit both a budget and this new ideal living place, California. Because the blocks are both decorative and structural, there are several different patterns cast into them, depending on where they are used. The patterns and variations also provide rhythm and texture to the design of the residence. The blocks have air space between them and are "knit" together with steel reinforcing. The air space provides insulation and helps to stabilize the temperatures inside.

The blocks were cast out of sand and material from the building site. Wright's reasoning for doing this is that it would make the residence more organic to its location. This idea of using materials from the site was not without its drawbacks. It was difficult to thoroughly clean the impurities from the sand used in casting the blocks, and over time, this has caused the blocks to deteriorate. The result is that this architectural gem of a cottage requires (and is currently receiving) restoration. The owner graciously allowed these photographs to be taken, but we were not able to make many interior images due to on-going construction.

top left: Stepped corner-framed windows eliminate the traditional junction of wall and glass.

center left: This narrow window/door allows access and ventilation while the glass brings the outdoors in — a Wright trademark.

bottom left: The two-story glass wall is separated from the floor of the balcony, allowing for a feeling of space and taking full advantage of the winter sun.

right: This window wall opens onto the balcony and overlooks a pond. The glass-filled perforated blocks above add light to both second and third floors.

132

Some of the blocks are pierced and have glass inserted to form both a contrasting pattern and allow for the interior to be light and airy but very private. Just off the patio to the west of the home is a reflecting pond and an artist's studio that was added later by Wright's son Lloyd, who also supervised the construction and landscaping.

La Miniatura was the first of four "block" residences that Frank Lloyd Wright built in California, but the others were of a much grander scale. Some of the others had guest cottages, but none currently remain, making La Miniatura the only California block cottage.

While the design of this cottage is a departure from the conventional ideas of a cottage, it remains faithful to the concept of small intimate spaces, compatibility with and connections to the environment, and low building costs. Instead of following traditional European cottage traditions for his inspiration, Wright relied upon his own aesthetics for a new American architecture. This cottage is an interesting contrast to appreciate the strength of the influence of European cottage traditions in other California cottages and Wright's new American architectural vision.

above: The main-floor fireplace is surrounded with different-patterned blocks as they are stepped back. By not using a flat wall on the sides of the fireplace, it gives the room a much larger feeling.

right: This detail of the fireplace shows the quality of light and shadow in the cottage.

left: Plantings and shadow gives a magic feel to this secluded home.

below: The rear of the home has a small reflecting pool with lush plantings that grow so well in Southern California's balmy climate.

MUSIC COTTAGE
REDLANDS

Redlands is in the part of California called the Inland Empire. It is sixty-five miles east of Los Angeles in San Bernardino County, and about 40 miles northwest of Palm Springs. The proximity to the Mojave Desert makes Redlands warm in the summer, sometimes reaching and passing 110°F. Early settlers found Redlands ideal for growing naval oranges and other citrus, and others came to Redlands for the warm dry climate for health reasons. It is the location of a private university, and the University of Redlands, and the city's cultural life prospered from the gifts of some noted philanthropists.

above: Topiaries, blooms, containers, reflecting balls, and garden art combine for a warm welcome to this 1925 cottage in Redlands.

left: The home's high gables and rounded-top doors are characteristic of an English cottage style which was popular in California between 1920 and 1940.

right: This side of the home has two levels with a bedroom and bath above the dining room and kitchen.

Ever since Joe Field and Jimmy Chagolla bought their home in Redlands, wonderfully strange occurrences have surprised them. Plates of cookies and boxes of fruit have arrived on the porch with anonymous notes saying "thanks for making my drive to work so beautiful," and strangers honk and wave. People started coming to the door with their stories, and from these, Field and Chagolla have pieced together the tale of their cottage.

One clipping they possess features a picture of their home on a July 1941 magazine cover that reads, "The Perfect Home."

While large for a cottage—1,100 square feet before a porch was enclosed and incorporated into the home—some proportions are small and intimate. The exception is the spacious living room. The home has a long horizontal reach paralleling the street, but a limited depth. This was explained by stories of the home. The house dates to 1925. The first occupants were

138

left: The unusually large size of the living room for a cottage allows for comfortable upholstered furniture and several conversation areas. The door at the right leads to a later room addition created by enclosing a porch.

right: This lovely window opens for cross-breezes.

below: Looking through the rounded-top doorway, the dining room is filled with greenery in true cottage style. The dining room is more typical of cottage proportions than the living room, which was designed larger for hosting musical recitals.

Miriam Scott and Flora Cook. Scott was an architectural drafter for Davis and Donald, an important development company in the Redlands area.

According to the stories, she designed the home herself and lived in a small one-room building in the back while she oversaw construction. Cook was a music teacher, and many visitors have described taking piano lessons in the home. Both were music lovers, and Scott designed the home anticipating concerts and planned for good acoustics, which explains the long rectangular shape of the living room and its high vaulted ceiling.

above: The mantel supports, stair railings, and balustrades are made from iron. The home owners kept with this material in their choices for the fireplace screen and curtain rods.

below: The low portion of the sloping gable covers an intimate entry furnished with a carved and mirrored hall tree. The entry floor is the same durable tile as used in the dining room.

There is an upstairs bedroom reached by a graceful curving stairway. On top of the stairway is a small landing. Here small string ensembles would play. A dining room is beneath the bedroom at the front of the home, while to the rear of the house is a kitchen.

Because of its original second purpose as a recital hall, the living room is larger than those of other cottages. This spaciousness allows for furnishing it with large upholstered pieces and to comfortably set up several conversation areas. Field and Chagolla have chosen traditional furniture in muted earth tones with eclectic antique and handmade accent pieces, collected art, plants, and delightful family photos.

The predominant shape of the home is a long rectangle with a slight "L" shape that is crowned with a sweeping front gable. The curving gable provides enough height for two stories and

right: The upstairs bedroom window repeats the curved pattern of the larger window downstairs. The angled bed solves the problems of working with windows and placing larger furniture in cottages and other small spaces.

left: The curving stairway is worthy of a descent by Loretta Young. String ensembles once performed on the upstairs landing. The downstairs doorway at the right leads to a tiled-floor dining room, and the doorway above leads to the bedroom.

gives the home the look of an English cottage. Between 1920 and 1940, the English cottage look was popular in California, and is identified by the steep roof and rounded-top doorways. This home repeats the rounded-top doorways also in the interior and in the windows. The style is an American version of a late Victorian English design that emulated rural vernacular cottages with some gothic influences. The home also has some iron detailing that is consistent with some Spanish Colonial Revival styles of the same period. The walls begin as masonry (concrete block) and transition to lathe and plaster. The thickness of the walls and the careful placement of windows for cross-ventilation keep the interior temperatures cool in the summer, although the owners are still grateful for some air conditioning.

Chagolla says that he has moved slowly in making any changes and improvements to the home, instead waiting until he is confident that what he does will suit the original design and aesthetics. It had previously been a rental for a number of years and was in need of maintenance and care. His neighbors sing his praises for the garden, and he admits that he moved in a load of mulch for the garden before any furniture for the house. The front is almost entirely blooming plants with the exception of a small grassy area. The home's lively beauty now stands out on the street, and cars slow down for a closer look. In keeping with the home's history as a musical venue, Field's and Chagolla's efforts to improve the home have received standing ovations.

REFERENCES & FURTHER READING

BOOKS

History of Art, H.W. Janson, 4th Edition, revised and expanded by Anthony F. Janson, 1991, Harry N. Abrams, Inc.

Creating Carmel: The Enduring Vision, Harold and Ann Gilliam, Gibbs Smith Books, 1992

Oxford Dictionary of Architecture, (Professor) James Stevens Curl, Oxford University Press, 1999

Los Angeles, An Architectural Guide, David Gebhard and Robert Winter, Gibbs Smith Publisher, 1994

Romanza: The California Architecture of Frank Lloyd Wright, David Gebhard, Chronicle Books, 1988

Cottages by the Sea: The Handmade Homes of Carmel, America's First Artist Community, Linda Leigh Paul, Universe Publishing (Rizzoli), 2000

The World Almanac and Book of Facts, 2001

Victorian Cottage Residences, Andrew Jackson Downing, Dover Publications, Inc., 1981

Late Victorian Houses and Cottages, Floor Plans and Illustrations for 40 House Designs, Designed by The Century Architectural Co., Dover Publications, Inc., 1999

American Victorian Cottage Homes by Palliser, Palliser & Co., Dover Publications, Inc., 1990

Discovering Cottage Architecture, Christopher Powell, Shire Publications, Ltd., 1996

The Not So Big House, A Blueprint for the Way We Really Live, Sarah Susanka, The Taunton Press, 2001

Creating the Not So Big House, Insights and Ideas for the New American Home, Sarah Susanka, The Taunton Press, 2000

Sierra Nevada Natural History, An Illustrated Handbook, Tracy I. Storer and Robert L. Usinger, University of California Press, 1963

The Tahoe Sierra, A Natural History Guide to 106 Hikes in the Northern Sierra, Jeffrey P. Schaffer, Wilderness Press, 1984

PUBLICATIONS

Historic Homes of Healdsburg, Second edition, A self-guided architectural and historic tour of homes, businesses, and churches, produced by volunteers of the Healdsburg Museum and Historical Society

Bungalow Heaven Home Tour 2002, brochure produced by the Bungalow Heaven Neighborhood Association, Pasadena, CA, including glossary

A Cottage is . . ., personal publication by Nadya Giusi, 2003, Carmel-by-the-Sea, CA

Pre-Railroad Farmhouse, personal publication by Dana Gene DiRicco, Healdsburg, CA

Los Angeles Times, July 21, 2002, Page K-1. *Mission Statement*, by Kathy Price-Robinson

WEBSITES

www.ragtime.org/arch/Arch_Cott
www.ci.alameda.ca.us/historical/architectural_styles-details
www.redlandsweb.com/history
www.pasadenahistory.org (Pasadena Museum of History)
www.monterey-carmel.com
www.sonomavalley.com/2000/bear_flag.htm
　　(Sonoma Valley Visitors Bureau)
www.sonomachalet.com
www.service.com/paw/Centennial/1994 (Palo Alto History)
www.millvalleyhistoricalsociety.org
www.census.abag.ca.gov/cities/MillValley
www.thecottageinn.com/tahoe
www.tahoeinfo.com/visit/history
www.gypsywheel.com (The art of J. Stengo & D. Gonzales)
www.historical.com/hollywood/history
www.hollywoodhistorymuseum.com

ABOUT THE AUTHORS

Scot Zimmerman has photographed architectural interiors, exteriors, and landscapes for over 25 years. In addition to work for private clients, his photographs have been featured in over 40 books, and his work regularly appears in many national and international publications.

Ann Getz Zimmerman is a planner and freelance writer with degrees in English, public administration, and dispute resolution. She writes about design, architecture, preservation, and art for a number of national and Utah publications. This is their second book collaboration.

The couple enjoys working and traveling together, and when they are not on the road, they live in an old farmhouse in Heber City, Utah.

ACKNOWLEDGMENTS

A book of this type relies upon the generosity and shared enthusiasm of home owners who will open their doors to a camera and disruption with little benefit to themselves. We were fortunate to find so many fine people who were willing to celebrate and share the special appeal of cottage living. We are also grateful to the many people who assisted us with this book by listening to us, making calls, and opening the first doors. Only with their help were we able to make photographs and research these projects. We would like to thank our dear friend Barbara Cannella for her knowledgeable comments, early edits, and encouragement. Finally, we express our appreciation to our editor, Laura Best, for her skill and commitment to this project and to the many capable and helpful people at Chapelle, Ltd., especially to Jo Packham who was first inspired to produce this book title.

On a personal note, I acknowledge my late grandmother, Sophie von Graufender Getz Schneider, for her many stories and loving nature and the curiosity and capacity for joy she inspired in all her grandchildren.

PLEASE ACCEPT OUR THANKS:

Borge Anderson & Associates
Rebecca Ittner
Peter O. Whitely
Kelly Schaefer
Jennifer Hathorne
Erika Kotite
Eileen Paulin
Mary & Bob Condry
Jan Ledgard
Carmel Cottage Society
Dirk Stennick
Drew Maran
Joe & Louise Tanous
Joe Leese
Dana DiRicco
Glenn Benjamin
Bob Kneisel
Carol Polanskey
Martin Ratliff
Manish Raval
Jana & Jim Gill
Enid Sales
Lois & Jack Prentice
Joan Barnes
Joe Field
Jimmy Chagolla
Kathy Frehner
Frank Herrendine
Redlands Historical Commission
Kathy Maddox
Janice Stengo
Daniel Gonzales
Chateau Marmount
Bob & Deedee Green
Carol Martinico

INDEX